r children's

we were tested

s journey end..."

"For as long as I live, I will never forget that in no other country on earth is my story even possible."

IN NO OTHER COUNTRY ON EARTH
PRESIDENT OBAMA

THE ROAD TO AN AMERICAN DREAM

INTRODUCTION BY JULIAN BOND

THE MCCLATCHY COMPANY

Published for The McClatchy Company
Sacramento, California
by Kansas City Star Books

First Edition
ISBN: 978-1-935362-00-5
Library of Congress Control Number: 2009921114

Editor: Monroe Dodd
Book designer: Jean Dodd

Dust jacket illustration:
Barrack Obama taking the oath of office as president, January 20, 2009 (Chuck Kennedy/MCT)

MCT: McClatchy/Tribune

Introductory photographs: Page 1: Obama approached the podium to speak at Fayetteville Technical Community College in North Carolina. (Shawn Rocco/The News & Observer, Raleigh). Page 3: At a rally after locking up the Democratic nomination, Nissan Pavilion, Bristow, Virginia, June 5, 2008. (Chuck Kennedy/MCT). Page 5: Taking oath of office as president, January 20, 2009 (Chuck Kennedy/MCT). Pages 7-8: The Capitol audience during the oath-taking. (Scott Andrews, pool/MCT).

Printed in the United States of America
by Walsworth Publishing Co. Inc., Marceline, Mo.

Credits for photo collage, pages 8-9

1. Michelle Bixby/*Centre Daily Times*, State College, Pennsylvania
2. Drew Perine/*The News Tribune*, Tacoma, Washington
3. Paul T. Erickson/*Tri-City Herald*, Kennewick, Washington
4. Travis Heying/ *The Wichita Eagle*, Kansas
5. Mike Ransdell/ *The Kansas City Star*, Missouri
6. Tim Isbell/*Sun Herald*, Gulfport, Mississippi
7. Danny Gawlowski/*The Bellingham Herald*, Washington
8. Corey Lowenstein/*The News & Observer*, Raleigh, North Carolina
9. Rex Babin/ *The Sacramento Bee*, California
10. Jason Vorhees/ *The Telegraph*, Macon, Georgia
11. Andy Burriss/*The Herald*, Rock Hill, South Carolina
12. Joe Jaszewski/ *Idaho Statesman*, Boise
13. Debbie Noda/*The Modesto Bee*, California
14. Corey Lowenstein/*The News & Observer*, Raleigh, North Carolina
15. C. Aluka Berry/*The State*, Columbia, South Carolina
16. Gary O'Brien/*The Charlotte Observer*, North Carolina
17. Tiffany Tompkins-Condie/ *Bradenton Herald*, Florida
18. Jeff Siner/*The Charlotte Observer*, North Carolina
19. Erik Hill/*Anchorage Daily News*, Alaska
20. Corey Lowenstein/*The News & Observer*, Raleigh, North Carolina
21. Ethan Hyman/*The News & Observer*, Raleigh, North Carolina
22. Jonathan Dyer/*The Island Packet*, Bluffton, South Carolina
23. David Perry/*Lexington Herald-Leader*, Kentucky
24. Randall Hill/*The Sun News*, Myrtle Beach, South Carolina
25. John Walker/*The Fresno Bee*, California
26. Tony Overman/*The Olympian*, Washington
27. Tiffany Tompkins-Condie/ *Bradenton Herald*, Florida

CONTENTS

By Julian Bond

Barack Obama's election as the first black president has caused great introspection and self-analysis by Americans and observers world-wide.

It has variously been credited as a repudiation of eight years of failed conservative government, the arrival of a post-civil rights era in American life, or the triumph of a canny candidate and the failure of his less competent opponents.

There's surely at least some small piece of each of these in Obama's victory, but to me it reflects something else as well. It has everything to do with the success of a transformative movement for equality that has struggled in the United States for more than a century. That movement can count Obama's election as one of its victories but cannot claim the final battle has been won or that race has been vanquished or that structural inequality and racist attitudes will end.

Even the election's good news is plagued by continuing incidents of racial animus that besmirch our ideals and repudiate the wishful predictions of a post-civil rights epoch for which many have longed. On election eve a gang of white youths in New York sought out blacks to assault in anger at Obama's victory. A coast away and a few weeks before the Inaugural a white policeman executed a black man whose arms were held behind his back. A new report confirms American schools are becoming more, not less, segregated.

None of this changes the fact that Obama's achievement is remarkable by any measure. Indeed, it reinforces it. This former community organizer ran the most organized political campaign in history. He won every age group under 65. He won a higher percentage of white men than any Democratic candidate since Jimmy Carter. He won among women by a 13 percent margin, among blacks by 96 percent, Hispanics by 67 percent and by 62 percent among Asians. He carried eight of the ten largest states and nine states that voted for George Bush in 2004. Three former Confederate states rejoined the Union, and with his election, our country rejoined the world community. Before November 4, we were a pariah state; in the aftermath we can begin to reclaim some of the esteem in which America once was held.

The Obama campaign did more than elevate a community organizer; it elevated community organizing and gave new prestige to a time-honored calling that has served the downtrodden, unrepresented and oppressed for centuries.

The political right, reeling from their rejection, has tried to cast the election as a center-right triumph. That is centrally wrong. Just as the 2006 midterm elections were a referendum on the war in Iraq — and the war lost, the 2008 election was a referendum on unfettered free market fundamentalism — and the free market lost. Those defeated could no longer defend the indefensible — low or no taxes for the wealthy, minimal or no regulation for the market, and an economy that does not respect work.

The spirit of Martin Luther King imbues any election, given the lasting importance of the Voting Rights Act of 1965, but King's spirit was especially evident in the momentous election of 2008. The Civil Rights Act of 1964 made discrimination based on race, gender, ethnicity, or religion illegal. Another act soon followed making discrimination based on age illegal. The major candidates in both side's primaries included a black man, a woman, a Hispanic, a Mormon, and a man, who became his party's nominee, who would have been the oldest person elected to the presidency. And in a first for his party, he chose a woman for his running mate.

All these candidates — and the nation — owe a debt to what the author Taylor Branch has called "the modern founders of democracy," those who labored, unknown and unheralded, in the vineyard of civil rights.

Dr. King's rhetorical dream of climbing the mountaintop does not mean the climb has ended for everyone else. Nor does Barack Obama's election mean the racial wars are won.

But it does mean that on November 5, 2008, we awakened to a new world where new possibilities beckoned and new realities reigned.

Julian Bond has been Chairman of the NAACP Board of Directors since February 1998. He is a Distinguished Scholar in the School of Government at American University in Washington, D.C., and a Professor in the Department History at the University of Virginia.

Julian Bond introduced Barack Obama at the annual NAACP national convention, July 14, 2008, in Cincinnati. (Al Behrman/Associated Press)

Capturing the moment

Since the beginning of the republic, presidential elections have galvanized Americans, and rarely more so than in times of national tribulation. When the presidential election season of 2008 began, the United States was in war abroad and in political tumult at home. By the time the year ended, the economy had spiraled downward.

Out of this discord arose a candidate who had spent only a brief time in the national spotlight, yet who took the nomination, the election and the country by storm.

Barack Obama defied conventional wisdom. Inexperience was supposed to count against him, and so was his color. He was an African-American in a country where no black person had ever won a major party nomination, let alone the presidency. Obama's remarkable victory, fueled by his eloquent message of unity, captured America's imagination.

On November 5, 2008, the day after the election, McClatchy Company newspapers from coast to coast headlined Obama's success. From city to city, copies sold out immediately. Even newspapers that increased their press runs could not satisfy the demand. Many returned to press and printed thousands of copies more.

From that phenomenal surge of interest arose the idea for this commemorative book. Using the work of scores of McClatchy reporters, photographers, artists and editors, it tracks the rise of Barack Obama from his debut on the national scene at the Democratic Convention in 2004 to his inauguration in 2009.

In No Other Country on Earth draws from eyewitness reports — each made as events unfolded — by journalists in the McClatchy Washington Bureau and at McClatchy newspapers across the United States. They covered the Obama campaign from the Carolinas to the Pacific, in New Hampshire villages and America's great cities. Through their talent and hard work, these journalists documented in words and images the wonders and the woes of the campaign, its successes and stumbles, and the spirit it created in millions of Americans.

Our title comes from Obama's speech on race in Philadelphia, March 18, 2008, a climactic period in his campaign.

"I have brothers, sisters, nieces, nephews, uncles and cousins, of every race and every hue, scattered across three continents," he said that day. "For as long as I live, I will never forget that in no other country on earth is my story even possible."

This is that story.

The editors

Hundreds of thousands braved the cold and filled the National Mall in Washington for Barack Obama's inauguration January 20, 2009. (Chuck Kennedy/MCT)

McClatchy Newspapers

ALASKA
Anchorage Daily News

CALIFORNIA
Merced Sun-Star
The Fresno Bee
The Modesto Bee
The Sacramento Bee
The Tribune, San Luis Obispo

FLORIDA
Bradenton Herald
The Miami Herald
El Nuevo Herald

GEORGIA
Ledger-Enquirer, Columbus
The Telegraph, Macon

IDAHO
Idaho Statesman, Boise

IILLINOIS
Belleville News-Democrat

KANSAS
The Wichita Eagle

KENTUCKY
Lexington Herald-Leader

MISSISSIPPI
Sun Herald, Gulfport

MISSOURI
The Kansas City Star

NORTH CAROLINA
The Charlotte Observer
The News & Observer, Raleigh

PENNSYLVANIA
Centre Daily Times

SOUTH CAROLINA
The Beaufort Gazette
The Herald, Rock Hill
The Island Packet, Bluffton
The State, Columbia
The Sun News, Myrtle Beach

TEXAS
Fort Worth Star-Telegram

WASHINGTON
The Bellingham Herald
The Olympian
The News Tribune, Tacoma
Tri-City Herald, Kennewick

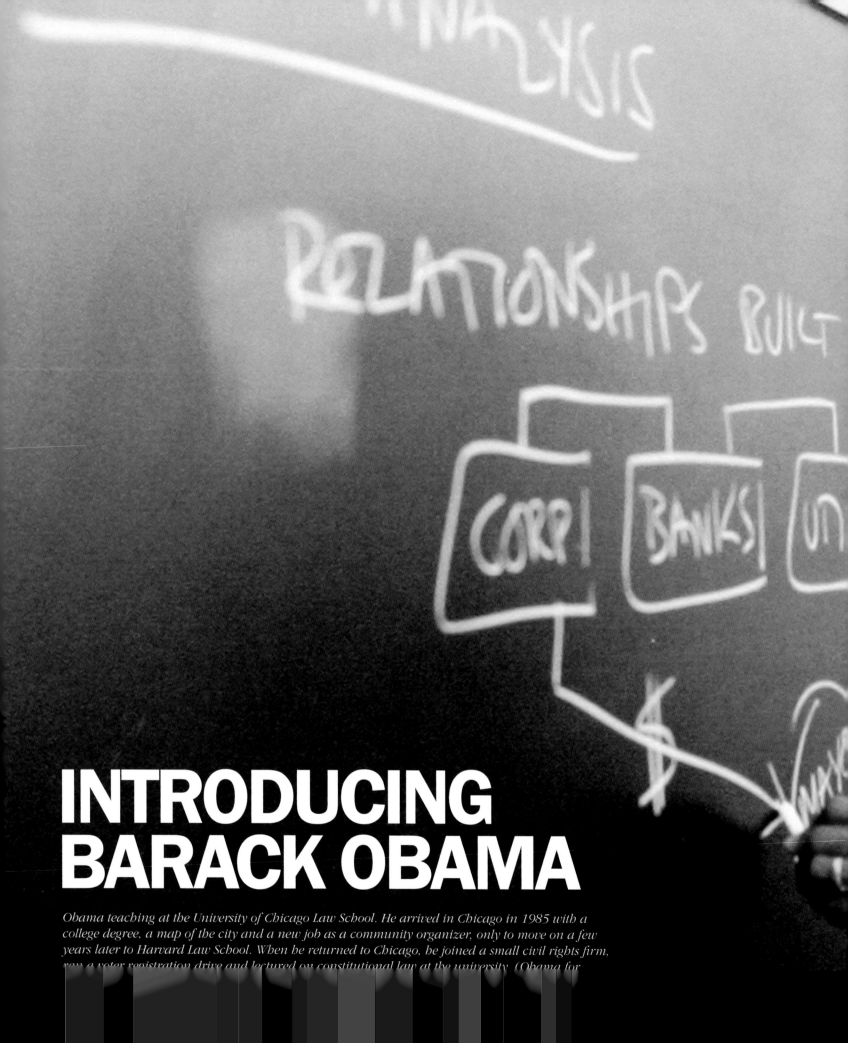

INTRODUCING
BARACK OBAMA

*Obama teaching at the University of Chicago Law School. He arrived in Chicago in 1985 with a
college degree, a map of the city and a new job as a community organizer, only to move on a few
years later to Harvard Law School. When he returned to Chicago, he joined a small civil rights firm,
ran a voter registration drive and lectured on constitutional law at the university. (Obama for*

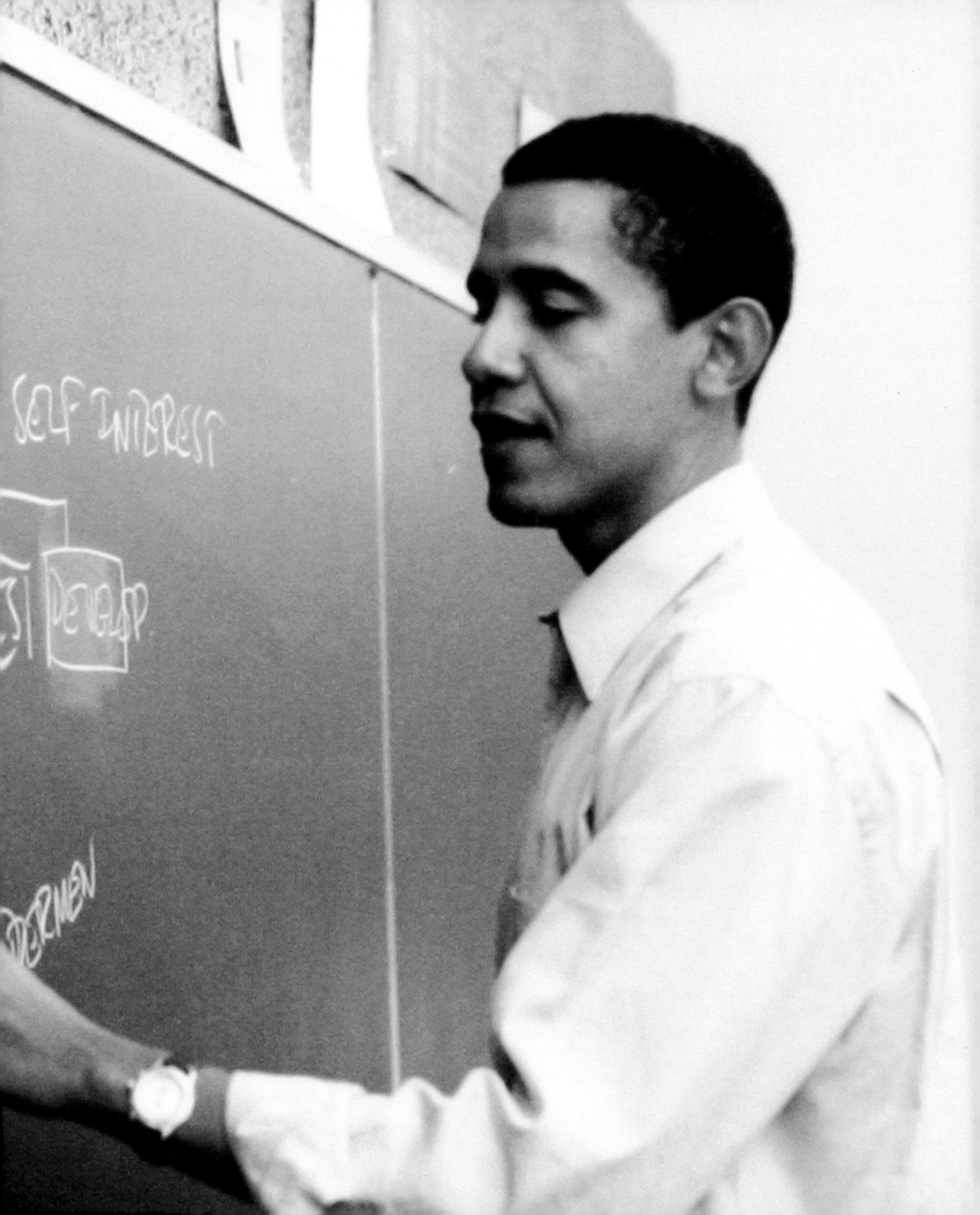
SELF INTEREST
DEVELOP

'An extraordinary man who speaks in an ordinary voice'

Springfield, Illinois: July 26, 2004

Tacked to a back wall of a storefront, recently converted into a campaign headquarters, is a 3-foot-high map of Illinois. It's topped with black lettering that declares: Obama Country.

Barack Obama, a 42-year-old Chicago law professor and an Illinois state senator, is all but a shoo-in to become the U.S. Senate's only black member, and only the third African-American senator since Reconstruction.

He's also scheduled to give the keynote address tomorrow night at the Democratic National Convention in Boston. Those who know Obama best say that after he finishes that speech, he'll gain serious national attention.

"He is the embodiment of exactly what a 21st-century candidate should be," says Janice Schakowsky, who represents most of Chicago's lakefront communities in Congress. "He crosses all kinds of lines, in part because of the person he is and in part because of his unifying message.

"He is an extraordinary man who speaks in an ordinary voice."

Blessed with matinee-idol looks, eloquence and

Those who know Obama best say that after he finishes that speech, he'll gain serious national attention.

charisma, Obama reached the edge of the national stage four months ago when he trounced six opponents in the Illinois Democratic primary for the U.S. Senate. The seat is open now that the Republican incumbent, Peter G. Fitzgerald, has announced he won't run.

Among those Obama defeated, with 52 percent of the vote, were a member of a Chicago political dynasty and a multimillionaire who spent more than $29 million of his own money. Obama attracted strong white suburban and rural support as well as black Chicagoans.

Nevertheless, when John Kerry, the soon-to-be nominee of the Democratic Party for president, invited Obama to speak at the convention, it was unexpected. Kerry called Obama "an optimistic voice for America."

"I was totally surprised and deeply honored," Obama said on a sweltering day last week at his campaign office here in the Illinois capital. He has been campaigning aggressively, but these days it is against no one in particular. His former Republican rival for the Senate seat, millionaire Jack Ryan, self-destructed last month when sordid details of his failed marriage came to light.

Easing his lanky frame into a folding chair, the sleeves of his crisp blue shirt rolled to the elbows, his tie barely loosened, Obama said he hadn't hesitated a moment in accepting Kerry's invitation.

After telling the news to his wife, Obama's next call was to his grandmother in Hawaii. That's where Obama's singular story began.

Obama's mother, a white woman born in Kansas, met his father, a member of a Kenyan tribe, when both were students at the University of Hawaii. They married in Maui in February 1961. Obama was born August 4, 1961, in Honolulu. Within a year Obama's father left to study at Harvard, intending eventually to return to Kenya. The couple divorced in 1964; both are now dead. In 1967 Obama's mother married an Indonesian businessman.

Obama spent much of his youth coming to grips with his biracial background, embracing his blackness without denying his white heritage. What helped in that difficult process were the glowing stories his mother and grandparents told about his father, a man who wrote often but met his son only once, when Obama was 10.

One such story, from Obama's 1995 memoir, *Dreams of My Father*, has his father unexpectedly faced with singing before hundreds of people. Having previously agreed to perform African folk songs for what he thought would be a small gathering, Obama's father nonetheless took to the stage and started singing.

"He wasn't great, but he was so sure of himself that before you knew it he was getting as much applause as anybody....Confidence. The secret to a man's success," wrote Obama, quoting his grandfather.

"My father would always say 'trust yourself.'"

Obama plans to speak to the Democrats about working hard to get ahead.

He's done that. After graduating from Columbia University in New York, Obama went to Chicago

One day before his keynote address to the 2004 Democratic National Convention in Boston, Obama spoke to the Black Caucus. (Chuck Kennedy/MCT)

to work with inner-city churches on community development. That sparked an interest in the law, and how it could be used to advance social change. He enrolled at Harvard Law School, where he was elected the first black president of the prestigious Harvard Law Review. Today he teaches constitutional law at the University of Chicago.

Emil Jones Jr., the Illinois state Senate president, calls Obama a consensus builder. He noted that Obama pushed through legislation that brought about dramatic death-penalty reforms in Illinois by persuading state prosecutors and police agencies to put aside their objections.

As Obama campaigns throughout Illinois, his appeal across racial lines is as obvious as it is sincere.

"When I'm in rural Illinois and see some elderly white couple, I see my grandparents," he says. "When I watch black girls playing Double Dutch on Chicago's South Side, those are my daughters."

Obama and his wife, Michelle, also a lawyer, have two young daughters.

The general election for Senate is three months away. Now the focus is on Boston.

"There is no doubt at all that he will do a terrific job," says Schakowsky, the congresswoman from Chicago.

She shares a story:

"I was at the White House with a congressional delegation and I reached out to shake hands with the president and he literally jumped back."

She could see that Bush had misread her "Obama" button.

"I carefully explained that it was Obama with a 'b' not an 's,' and that he was running for senator. The president said, 'I don't know him.'

"After Tuesday night, he's sure going to know who he is."

— *Carl Chancellor/Knight Ridder*

Following pages: Facing a sea of signs promoting his candidacy for the Senate from Illinois, Obama prepared to give the convention keynote address. (Chuck Kennedy/KRT)

Delegates to the 2004 Democratic Convention awaited the next speaker on July 27. (Saul Loeb/KRT)

His night on the big stage

Boston: July 27, 2004

Speaking with passion that often touched on lofty themes, the fresh new face of Barack Obama tonight summoned the Democratic Party to its highest ideals while also condemning the Bush Administration.

"There's not a liberal America and a conservative America ... a black America and white America and Latino American and Asian America," he said. "There's the United States of America."

Obama said his parents "would give me an African name, Barack, or 'blessed,' believing that in a tolerant America, your name is no barrier to success."

He called for a government compassionate in deeds as well as words.

"People don't expect government to solve all of their problems," he said. "But they sense, deep in their bones, that with just a slight change in priorities, we can make sure that every child in America has a decent shot at life and that the doors of opportunity remain open to all."

An opponent of the war in Iraq, Obama referred emotionally and with partisanship to the responsibilities that accompanied power.

"When we send our young men and women into harm's way, we have a solemn obligation not to fudge the numbers or shade the truth about why they're going," he said. "To care for their families while they're gone. To tend to the soldiers upon their return, and to never, ever, go to war without enough troops to win the war, secure the peace and earn the respect of the world."

He called for greater compassion for all Americans, especially those under intense pressure.

"If there's an Arab-American family being rounded up without benefit of an attorney or due process, that threatens my civil liberties," he said. "It's that fundamental belief — I am my brother's keeper, I am my sister's keeper — that makes this country work."

Obama, a dynamic speaker who was the star of the show, delivered the keynote address in prime time but no one watching ABC, CBS or NBC could see it. All three major networks decided not to broadcast any of tonight's proceedings live, leaving that to some cable and public broadcasting operations. Television ratings for last night's opening session dropped by 10 percent from the same event four years ago.

— Martin Merzer/The Miami Herald

Joined by his wife, Michelle, Obama acknowledged cheers for his 17-minute convention speech, which turned him in one night from an unknown to a political star. (Charlie Neibergall/Associated Press)

Instantly, the buzz runs Obama's way

Boston: July 28, 2004

His name is hard to remember, but many here won't soon forget him.

Barack Obama had Democratic convention delegates buzzing today about the eventual possibility of seeing him as the nation's first African-American president.

"Wow! It was a phenomenal speech!" exclaimed David Kahn, a delegate from Portland, Oregon, over the thumping music at an after-party honoring the Democrats' rising star. Kahn and many others left the convention hall impressed. Within hours, they were citing the speech almost word for word: "There's not a liberal America and a conservative America. There's the United States of America."

In the crush of well-wishers at his after-party at the fashionable Vinalia restaurant in downtown Boston, Obama was barely able to take two steps at a time as he moved across the room. Supporters cheered the rock-star politician who captivated audiences with his story of a "skinny boy with a funny name who believes that America has a place for him, too."

He wouldn't talk about his long-term ambitions, but there were plenty of people ready to dream big dreams for him.

"If anyone can do it, Obama can," said a hopeful Artur Davis, a congressman from Alabama who studied at Harvard Law School when Obama served as the first black president of the *Harvard Law Review*.

"Obama may help break down the stereotypes that an African-American politician is someone only for other blacks," said Davis, who is black. "He has the capacity to run as a candidate for everyone."

He proved he could cut across racial and geographic divides in the Illinois state primary for Senate, where the Chicagoan won his home turf, the white suburbs and southern counties.

— *Sumana Chatterjee/Knight Ridder*

Mania for 'it' man

Boston: July 29, 2004

The young pols stood up and hollered as U2's "Beautiful Day" blared. When Sean "P. Diddy" Combs walked in, they shouted their love and refused to sit down, even as the icon of coolness implored them to take a load off.

But if you want to know who was the No. 1 star among Generation Y types at the Democratic National Convention this week, look no farther than the once-obscure state senator from Illinois: Barack Obama.

His keynote address electrified the convention, served notice that a new star was born and triggered a wave of Obamamania. Obama is almost certain to win election to the U.S. Senate in November, and if so, he'll become only the third black person elected to the Senate since Reconstruction.

At the Youth Caucus, Democratic devotees called Obama the biggest celebrity, the hottest ticket, the fastest-rising personality in Boston.

"He will be the first black president of the United States," said Jonny Sonquist, 20, a Democratic campaigner from Minneapolis who visited the Democrats' Youth Caucus today. "I am so absolutely in love with him."

A volunteer for a public-interest group, Mark Greenbaum, 24, of South Orange, New Jersey, said Obama's charisma helped him connect.

Obama also scores big with his multicultural background, clear intellect and Harvard Law degree.

Whatever the "it" is, Obama has it.

The Democratic Colin Powell? The new Bill Clinton? All comparisons were fair game among young activists. Obama was the king buzz-maker of any Boston party he attended.

"The response of young voters has been overwhelming," said Kouri Marshall, Obama's voter-outreach coordinator. Chatting outside the Youth Caucus, Marshall said the week had been like "one big party" and that "the Republicans better watch out."

Pressed about suggestions that Obama could become an unstoppable presidential contender in 2008 or 2012, Marshall said: "Obama is a step-by-step man. He's focused on the Senate seat."

— *Adam Smeltz/Knight Ridder*

On the eve of election day 2004, Obama took his campaign for the U.S. Senate to Granite City, Illinois. (Derik Holtmann/Belleville News-Democrat.)

The senator-elect from Illinois

Victory secure on election night in 2004, the Obamas held their daughters, Malia, left, and Sasha as a storm of confetti surrounded them in Chicago. (M. Spencer Green/Associated Press)

Chicago: November 2, 2004

Barack Obama, who catapulted onto the national stage with a stirring speech at the Democratic National Convention, today easily won election as the new U.S. senator from Illinois. He will be the only African-American in that body.

He handily beat Republican challenger Alan Keyes, a conservative talk-show host who never mustered much support. Obama had faced a potentially tough contest until his opponent, Republican Wall Street investment banker Jack Ryan, withdrew in the face of reports about his personal life. Obama won a commanding 70 percent of the votes to Keyes' 27 percent.

Virtually assured of victory for months, Obama lent his telegenic appeal and donated excess campaign funds to other Democrats in the fall campaign.

Obama ran a multicultural, moderate campaign, painting himself as a mainstream politician for all people. As the Illinois state senator, he represented Chicago's south side, focusing on housing, education and health care. Some think the Senate is only the next step for Obama and are looking for his name on a future presidential ticket.

A mother from Kansas, a father from Kenya

Five years before giving birth to a future political star, the girl from Kansas extended her hand to Susan Botkin, a fellow ninth-grader.

"Hi. I'm Stanley," she said, rolling her eyes. "My dad wanted a boy."

Convention rarely fit Stanley Ann Dunham.

Obama likes to talk about her Kansas roots, repeating "mother from Kansas, father from Kenya," implying the values of the heartland in the parent who stuck by him. But Stanley Ann Dunham hardly left a trace in the Sunflower State, where she was born. Her family swept through California and Texas before returning briefly to El Dorado, Kansas, her dad's hometown, when she was in seventh grade.

The Dunhams soon left the heartland for good. And from the islands where she spent her remaining 40 years until her death from ovarian cancer in 1995, she never looked back.

The girl from Kansas twice entered into wedlock, once with a Kenyan and once with an Indonesian; both marriages broke apart. She studied anthropology and spent years in Indonesia, teaching English and lining up microloans for the poor.

She spoke Javanese, French, Indonesian and a bit of Urdu.

And she trusted her son, "Barry," to overcome the thorny identity issues of a childhood without a father.

He did. Barack Obama found his path to a prestigious college — even as his mom pursued interests half a world away. He later attributed "what is best in me" to her can-do idealism and resilience to adversity. He also noted how her wanderlust and "a certain recklessness" compelled him to seek for his own daughters a more stable upbringing — a home in Chicago, with two parents.

Those who knew her noticed other traits passed down to Obama: A pointy chin, tilted up in pensive moments. A genuine rejection of racial lines. A supreme confidence — some might say elitism — in the face of circumstances that were anything but elite.

"She provided a very different role" from other mothers of her day, said Susan Blake, the former Susan Botkin.

Most of what is known about Stanley Ann Dunham's childhood comes from her son's 1995 memoir, *Dreams From My Father*, which she proofread before she died.

She was born in November 1942 at Fort Leavenworth, Kansas, to Stan and Madelyn Dunham — both Kansas natives from the "dab-smack, landlocked center of the country," Obama wrote.

Her father was a restless furniture salesman who so desired a son that he gave his daughter his first name. He joined the Army shortly

Obama in Collinsville, Illinois. (Zia Nizami/Belleville News-Democrat)

after the attack on Pearl Harbor and probably was off to war when his wife traveled from the Wichita area to give birth.

Leavenworth post historian Kelvin Crow explains: "It's reasonable to believe that's why she'd be born here — for the medical benefits."

Obama's mother spent her infancy in the Wichita area, where mother Madelyn worked during World War II at a B-29 bomber factory. Later, in Texas, according to Obama's book, an 11-year-old Stanley Ann endured teasing from neighbors after she invited a black child into her yard to play. By the mid-1950s, if just for one year, the family was in El Dorado, according to records in the Kansas town.

Before 1956, when the Dunhams again left Kansas, Stanley Ann hadn't stayed in one place long enough to leave much of an impression.

That changed on Mercer Island, Washington, where classmate Jill Burton-Dascher said: "She was comfortable in the bohemian group. They spent a lot of time in coffeehouses."

Graduates of the Mercer Island class of 1960 reckon that Stanley Ann's mother, of white-collar stock and now a bank executive, persuaded her freewheeling husband to settle down for the sake of their daughter's education.

That education included questioning authority and religious institutions, and reading the works of Marx and Kierkegaard. Friend John Hunt recalled that Stanley Ann "could step into a conversation and lightly call someone to account. She wasn't nasty, but neither was she intimidated."

When she graduated, the Dunhams moved to Hawaii, where she applied to a university and quickly fell in love with one of the few black students on campus.

Barack Obama Sr. was Kenyan, deep-voiced, well-spoken and viewed by many female students as an exotic catch.

Alice Dewey, a friend, said: "He had whatever that spark is, the spark his son has today."

"He was brilliant," said Rep. Neil Abercrombie of Hawaii, a fellow graduate student.

Stanley Ann Dunham was 18 and pregnant when she married, to the disapproval of her parents. Friends wondered whether her relationship with a black man was meant to shock her father. But all doubts dissipated when she passed through Mercer Island in 1961 with her month-old son.

"She was so proud of her baby, so relaxed, so self-possessed — excited about the future," said Blake, who changed Barry's diaper.

The Dunham-Obama marriage failed within three years.

The elder Obama returned to Kenya to pursue politics but became embittered by the tribal order. He had little contact with his ex-wife and son, though she never spoke a harsh word to Barry about his father except that he was a bad driver. (He died in a traffic accident in 1982.)

In Hawaii, Stanley Ann had re-enrolled at the university to study anthropology.

For a time, she received food stamps.

By 1967 she had married an Indonesian student, Lolo Sotoroe, and followed him to his country. They lived in a house lacking electricity and a bathtub. There, Barry acquired a half-sister, Maya Sotoroe.

"My mom's optimism might be seen as naive, but it informed my brother's politics in a very significant way," she says.

He attended a Catholic school, where the Indonesian kids called him "Negro."

His mother, always the educator, woke him at 4 a.m. for American correspondence courses.

She showered Barry with books about the U.S. civil rights movement, speeches of Martin Luther King Jr. and recordings of Mahalia Jackson.

"To be black was to be the beneficiary of ... a special destiny, glorious burdens that only we were strong enough to bear," Obama wrote. "More than once my mother would point out: 'Harry Belafonte is the best-looking man on the planet.'"

When Barry turned 10, she recognized the limitations of his Indonesian education. She and the children returned to Hawaii so he could attend the prestigious Punahou prep school. When her fondness for Indonesia pulled, she allowed Barry to stay in Honolulu. Her parents finished the job of raising him. Hawaii's multi-ethnic culture granted young Barry "a freedom" that mixed-race children wouldn't enjoy in other places, Abercrombie said.

Grandfather Stan, who died in 1992, finally had the boy he'd hoped for. His daughter opened a school in Jakarta teaching English and helped build an Indonesian program that provided tiny loans to entrepreneurs with poor credit.

Fellow anthropologist Dewey recalls her motto, "'Gee, Toto, I don't think we're in Kansas anymore.' And wouldn't you know? Little Dorothy just takes over."

The son had graduated from Harvard Law School and was close to launching his political career in Illinois when cancer claimed his mom in 1995. Among his biggest regrets, he says, was not being at her bedside when she died in Hawaii.

— *Rick Montgomery/The Kansas City Star*

A village in Africa

Nairobi, Kenya: August 28, 2006

Barack Obama Sr. and Stanley Ann Dunham in the early '70s. (AP/Obama for America)

Son Barack with his father. (AP/Obama for America)

Obama and maternal grandparents Stanley Armour Dunham and Madelyn Lee Payne Dunham in New York City (AP Photo/ Obama for America)

At the midpoint of a two-week swing with his family through Africa, Barack Obama is paying a four-day visit to Kenya, the country where his father was born. He has been greeted like a head of state or a sports legend, not like a freshman U.S. senator.

Kenyans have eagerly embraced Obama since 2004, when he was elected as the U.S. Senate's only African-American. Speculation since has grown that he'll one day run for president. Children here have been named for him — in Swahili his first name means "blessing" — as have countless schools and businesses in the rural western region from where his family hails. The locally brewed Senator beer is now better known as "Obama" — a high honor in this land of big drinkers.

Obama's father, once a Kenyan goat herder who became an economist, died in a car accident in Kenya in1982. Obama's paternal grandmother and about 30 other family members still live in the village of Kogelo, which Obama first visited in 1987 before he entered Harvard Law School.

With his wife and two daughters Obama returned to the village of his father's humble beginnings. A carnival atmosphere prevailed. Onlookers climbed trees and lampposts or balanced atop bicycles to glimpse Obama. Vendors hawked T-shirts with his image and the message, "We are proud you are a Kenyan."

Obama didn't disappoint, issuing a brief greeting in the language of his father's Luo tribe, which sent the crowd of thousands into wild cheers.

He also shared brief memories of his father, whom he has said he didn't know well.

"Whenever I see a young boy 5 or 6 or 7 or 10, I think about my father," Obama said. "I think about the journey he traveled so many miles over such a great distance. I think of those young boys and I think there is no reason why they can't do the same."

Obama shared a tight embrace with his 80-year-old paternal grandmother, Sarah Hussein Obama, who held him by the waist as she took him on a tour of his cousins' houses.

"I am very happy especially seeing his children," said his grandmother, wearing a yellow floral-print African dress and headscarf. "He is a kid who belongs to this homestead."

—*Shashank Bengali, Munene Kilongi/McClatchy*

Part memoir, part politics, part chutzpah

Washington, D.C.: October 20, 2006

If the title of Sen. Barack Obama's new book, *The Audacity of Hope: Thoughts on Reclaiming the American Dream*, sends you page-turning in search of daring solutions for the nation's problems, you may feel let down. But if you're one of many Americans who see the eloquent 45-year-old biracial senator from Illinois as a player to watch in future presidential politics, his second memoir offers some intimate glimpses into the man on the pedestal.

Its timing and chutzpah are certain to raise some eyebrows. For all the buzz about Obama, being a junior senator in the party out of power hasn't allowed him to accomplish much yet. Only one of his bills has been enacted into law — creating a database so the public can track federal contracts — and it had a Republican co-sponsor, Sen. Tom Coburn of Oklahoma.

Despite that, the book's release this month comes at a pivotal time: just before elections in

> Right off the bat, President Bush pulls him aside to warn him, "You've got a bright future. ... Everybody'll be waiting for you to slip ... so watch yourself."

which Democrats are trying to recapture the House of Representatives and the Senate, and as politicians who are considering presidential runs start getting serious.

Obama, who's said he's not planning to run for president in 2008, nevertheless made his first appearance last month in Iowa — where the first balloting for 2008 candidates occurs — as a speaker at Democratic Sen. Tom Harkin's annual steak-fry. And he's stumping for Democrats in congressional races all over the country.

The Audacity of Hope is the first installment of a three-book deal that Obama inked before he took office. It focuses on his experiences on the campaign trail, during his breakthrough speech at the 2004 Democratic National Convention and in his first two years in the Senate. The second installment is to be a children's book, not yet written, and the theme of the third isn't set.

"I'm not sure anything's more audacious than thinking I could actually write a book while I was serving in the Senate," he joked in a hurried phone interview. The book is part history, part political platform and part memoir; the latter carries the book.

A freshly sworn-in Obama takes the reader onto the Senate floor, peeling back the pomp to expose the reality in which politicians typically demagogue to TV cameras in an otherwise empty chamber: "In the world's greatest deliberative body, no one is listening."

He writes of his poignant first meeting with Democratic Sen. Robert Byrd of West Virginia, the 88-year-old orator and master of Senate rules who joined the Ku Klux Klan as a young man but later regretted it. He rubs shoulders with Google executives and billionaire investor Warren Buffett, but also with poor women and union workers struggling with family health crises and lost jobs. He worries that the social perks and time constraints of his job could conspire to insulate him from the masses and change his sense of self. At moments he comes across as aloof.

There's a revelation of self-doubt: Is he battle-ready, given that his ascent from state lawmaker to senator was eased by his opponents' flameouts?

"To political insiders my victory proved nothing," he wrote of his 2004 election. "No wonder then that upon my arrival in Washington that January (of 2005), I felt like the rookie who shows up after the game, his uniform spotless, eager to play, even as his mud-splattered teammates tend to their wounds."

He reveals ambition, posturing and humility.

Right off the bat, President Bush pulls him aside to warn him, "You've got a bright future. ... Everybody'll be waiting for you to slip ... so watch yourself."

Obama subtly positions himself to red-state voters:

He says the publicity wave after his 2004 convention speech "reinforces my sense of how fleeting fame is, contingent as it is on a thousand different matters of chance, of events breaking this way rather than that."

He wrote of falling in love with his wife, recalling that their first kiss "tasted of chocolate."

Some of the book's most eloquent moments are

Autograph-seekers stood by with copies of The Audacity of Hope *when Obama spoke at a Democratic rally November 5, 2006, in Collinsville, Illinois. (Zia Nizami/Belleville News-Democrat)*

in Obama's discussion of Americans' race relations and the struggles of black Americans. Nestled in these passages are the gambles on which his future political opportunities may be built.

Obama asserts that "the overwhelming majority of white Americans these days are able — if given the time — to look beyond race in making their judgments of people.

"That simple notion — that one isn't confined in one's dreams — is so central to our understanding of America that it seems almost commonplace. It is

perhaps the most important legacy of the civil rights movement."

Only in the book's epilogue does Obama answer one nagging question: The book's title is borrowed from his pastor, who's used the phrase to describe the power of the human spirit to persevere despite hardships and obstacles.

— Margaret Talev/
McClatchy Washington Bureau

Not yet a candidate, but drawing crowds

Manchester, New Hampshire:
December 10, 2006

Barack Obama shook up the embryonic 2008 presidential campaign today, igniting a tumultuous response in his first visit to the state that will kick off primary voting for the 2008 Democratic nomination in about a year.

More than 1,500 Democrats crowded into a Manchester armory to see and hear the freshman senator, a turnout that local organizers called unprecedented this long before the voting.

The armory crowd roared its approval when Gov. John Lynch speculated that Obama might run, and they interrupted the senator's half-hour speech several times with ovations. His speech focused on forging a bipartisan civil approach to solving problems in education, healthcare and national security. That amounts to "an American agenda," he said, not a partisan one.

Earlier today, more than 700 showed up to see him at a Portsmouth book signing, forcing the event to

> ### "That my 15 minutes of fame has extended somewhat is surprising to me and baffling to my wife."

be moved from a bookstore to a conference center.

The Illinois senator hasn't even decided yet whether to run. And not all who showed up to hear him would necessarily vote for him. But the intense curiosity and enthusiasm about him among Democrats suggests that the party is looking for new leadership — and that the presumed frontrunner, Hillary Rodham Clinton, is anything but a certain winner.

"We've never had an event like this," said New Hampshire Democratic Party Chairwoman Kathy Sullivan.

The $25 tickets sold out in a blur of advance demand, and party officials posted signs warning people there wasn't room for anyone else.

More than 150 members of the news media, including foreign press, covered Obama's arrival. Candidates at this stage of a campaign normally consider themselves lucky to draw four or five reporters.

By comparison, another potential 2008 Democratic candidate who's been visiting New Hampshire frequently went largely unnoticed at a simultaneous visit. Sen. Evan Bayh of Indiana ate breakfast all but anonymously with two other people this morning in a restaurant next door to the Obama event. The evening before, he hosted a reception that drew about 50 Democrats.

For his part, Obama claimed humility.

"I'm suspicious of hype," Obama said upon arriving in Manchester. "That my 15 minutes of fame has extended somewhat is surprising to me and baffling to my wife."

But he said his civil approach, which he calls "a hopeful politics," might be striking a chord with Americans weary of partisan sniping and gridlock in Washington.

"People are very hungry for something new," he said. "To some degree, I am a stand-in for that desire."

Indeed, many Democrats noted that they liked the fact that he's a newcomer to national politics, with just two years in the Senate.

"We're looking for somebody new," said Carol Williams of Manchester. "People are tired of the same old stuff, the same old politics. All the rest of them are part of the old boy, old girl network.

"Barack is eloquent and charismatic. He has the same charisma as John Kennedy," she said. "I know; I worked for him here in 1960."

She wasn't the only one who likened Obama to President Kennedy.

"He's passionate and he's young. It's a Jack Kennedy thing," said Carol Backus of Manchester.

If Obama exudes a JFK-like charisma for some, he doesn't share Kennedy's 14 years of pre-presidential experience in Congress. Some Democrats said they didn't mind his lack of experience; others said it would be a significant hurdle.

"The pedigree is important, but the ability to connect to people is more important," said state Sen. Lou D'allesandro of Manchester. "He's a very attractive candidate."

A new national poll last week showed Clinton ahead in the early jockeying for the Democratic nomination, but trailing either Republican Rudy Giuliani or John McCain in a hypothetical general election.

Clinton had the support of 33 percent of Democrats for their party's nomination, according to the Marist

New Hampshire Democrats packed an armory in Manchester to hear Obama on December 10, 2006. It was the senator's first visit to the state, which every four years holds the first presidential primary. (Jim Cole,/Associated Press)

College-WNBC poll. Former Sen. John Edwards of North Carolina had 14 percent, former Vice President Al Gore had 13 percent, Obama had 12 percent, and Sen. John Kerry of Massachusetts had 5 percent.

An X factor is Obama's race — he would be the first African-American presidential nominee of either major party.

"Race is still a powerful force," he acknowledged today, but he said he was optimistic.

Obama also said he didn't think his middle name, Hussein, would be a problem. If names were a problem, he said with a smile, voters would never get past his first name.

"When you're already starting with Barack ..." he said with a laugh.

— *Steven Thomma/*
McClatchy Washington Bureau

Race: Presenting a higher threshold

Manchester, New Hampshire:
December 12, 2006

As it often does for a politician with dark skin, the subject turned to race when Barack Obama arrived in one of the whitest states in the union last weekend.

"Race is still a powerful force in this country," the freshman Democratic senator from Illinois told a horde of reporters and television crews. "Any African-American candidate, or any Latino candidate, or Asian candidate, or woman candidate confronts a higher threshold in establishing himself to the voters."

Yet he added that he believed the country had changed, grown more tolerant, quicker to get past race and onto the business of judging politicians on their characters and visions. Should he decide to run for president, he said, "people will know me pretty well, and whether I'm qualified to serve or not."

As if to underscore the point, Obama received a rock star's welcome when he appeared an hour later before an eager crowd of more than 1,500, the overwhelming majority of them white. They cheered his speech, roared approval at the suggestion that he might run and crowded around him afterward, reaching out to touch him or take a picture.

Obama hasn't decided whether to run. But the intense interest in him suggests that he'd be the first African-American in history with a real shot at winning not only a major party nomination but perhaps the presidency as well.

The person he'd have to get past is probably Hillary Clinton, who'd have a real chance of becoming the first woman to win a major party nomination or the White House.

Obama has cross-racial appeal. He's a politician who happens to be black, not a black politician. One elderly New Hampshire Democrat told me that Obama's race made him more appealing: "His skin color is a novelty." Another said it would feel good as a Democrat to vote for a minority.

Yet most seemed to ignore his race altogether—at least they didn't mention it.

That's far different from the reaction to other black candidates, such as Jesse Jackson or Al Sharpton.

"America is ready to elect a black president," Vanderbilt University political scientist Carol Swain writes for next month's issue of *Ebony* magazine. "But the first successful black president will not be a Jesse Jackson or an Al Sharpton or any veteran activist of the Civil Rights Movement. Such a candidate laden with heavy baggage would evoke too much white guilt, and he or she would be seen more as a 'black' candidate than one who happened to be black."

Rather, she writes, the first black president will be someone who embodies a broader vision of hope, such as Obama or former Secretary of State Colin Powell. "It will be a person who ascribes to the mainstream political and social values that place heavy emphasis on hard work and individual responsibility."

That's the way that Harold Ford, an African-American Democrat, campaigned for a Senate seat in Tennessee. He stressed religious faith and his devotion to his family, even though his family drew criticism for allegations of corruption.

Although Ford lost, 51-48 percent, he came closer than polls had suggested. Only 16 percent of Tennessee's population is black. More important, his election day support from whites matched what pre-election polls had predicted. That's a reversal from the long history of whites telling pollsters they would support black candidates, then voting against them.

"There is a lot of evidence that under the right circumstances, Americans really connect with and embrace people of color, especially people who represent the core common values of hard work and opportunity," Democratic pollster Geoff Garin said.

He noted that some of the most trusted people in the country today were African-Americans, including TV host Oprah Winfrey, Secretary of State Condoleezza Rice and Powell.

"While both African-Americans and women candidates have a special burden of proof," he said, "it is achievable."

— Steven Thomma/
McClatchy Washington Bureau

A short-timer, yet ready to run

Trailed by a flock of photographers, Obama jogged up the Capitol steps on his way to a Senate vote on January 15, 2007. A day later, he filed papers signaling his interest in running for president. (Chuck Kennedy/MCT)

Washington, D.C.: January 16, 2007

Barack Obama today took the first step toward seeking the presidency, filing papers with the Federal Election Commission that allowed him to form a committee to raise money and hire staff

The move propelled him into the top tier for the 2008 Democratic presidential nomination and put him in position to test how much his party and his country hunger for change.

Just 45 years old and two years into his first term in the Senate, Obama brings to the campaign the prospect of a new generation and style of leadership, with less experience in Washington and far fewer ties to the political polarization of the past two decades there.

He has scheduled a formal announcement of his candidacy for February 10.

In a statement, Obama lamented that "our leaders in Washington seem incapable of working together in a practical, commonsense way. Politics has become so bitter and partisan, so gummed up by money and influence, that we can't tackle the big problems that demand solutions."

Obama's youth and lack of experience in Washington are, at once, among his strongest assets and most glaring weaknesses. Yet while many politicians in similar circumstances invoke the youthful John F. Kennedy, watch for Obama to conjure up a bolder comparison: Abraham Lincoln.

Obama's formal declaration of candidacy will come two days before Lincoln's birthday—in the Illinois

Collegial greeting: Sen. John McCain of Arizona shook hands with Obama before the Illinois senator testified at a hearing on global warming on Capitol Hill January 30, 2007. (Chuck Kennedy/MCT)

Bill Richardson is expected to announce his candidacy later this month. All score lower in early polls than Clinton, Obama and Edwards.

So far, being the new face with the new message of bipartisan cooperation has helped Obama, particularly as many Democrats have soured on Washington politicians who endorsed the Iraq war at the outset and might be portrayed as too ingrained in Washington to change.

Indeed, Obama sought to use his short time in Washington to his advantage, distancing himself from the partisan politics that many Americans despise and subtly criticizing fellow Democrats for going along. It also was noteworthy that he didn't criticize President Bush by name, a staple of Democratic politics.

He disappointed some Democrats when he appeared Sunday on CBS's "Face the Nation" and sidestepped questions about whether he'd support cutting off money to force an end to the Iraq war.

Obama also faces other challenges and questions, including his race. Yet in an age when Tiger Woods leads pro golf, Oprah Winfrey dominates the airwaves, and Colin Powell and Condoleezza Rice take turns as the country's chief diplomat, those barriers might be falling. While Obama doesn't shy from his heritage, he doesn't want to be marginalized as a "black candidate" who appeals primarily to black voters.

That's part of the rationale for launching his campaign in Springfield, according to Illinois Democrats who spoke on condition of anonymity because they weren't authorized to speak for the campaign. A speech on the South Side of Chicago could draw an overwhelmingly black audience. A Springfield event would draw a more diverse group.

Those pushing for Springfield gave two other reasons:

• It would draw attention to Obama's seven years in the Illinois Senate before his election to the U.S. Senate. His campaign aides have found that focus groups of voters were favorably impressed with his time in the Illinois legislature, a possible counter to complaints that his two years in Congress leave him too inexperienced.

• It could invite comparisons to Lincoln, who served eight years in the Illinois legislature. And Lincoln served only two years in Congress, two less than Obama will have served by Inauguration Day 2009.

— *Steven Thomma/
McClatchy Washington Bureau*

state capital of Springfield, where he and Lincoln both served, rather than his hometown of Chicago.

Obama approaches the campaign with polls showing him in the top ranks of a largely open race for his party's nomination, along with Hillary Clinton and John Edwards.

Obama is competitive in each of the first four states that are scheduled to vote for a Democratic nominee next year—he's running fourth in Iowa, second in Nevada, second in New Hampshire and third in South Carolina—according to recent polls by the American Research Group. Clinton leads in all four states, but she commands only about a third of total support. She's expected to declare her intentions soon.

Other announced Democratic candidates include Sens. Christopher Dodd of Connecticut and Joseph Biden of Delaware, Gov. Tom Vilsack of Iowa and Rep. Dennis Kucinich of Ohio. New Mexico's Gov.

Joseph Biden, chairman of the Senate Foreign Relations Committee, presided over a hearing in January 2007. (Chuck Kennedy/MCT)

Biden: Out of the gate, with a misstep

Washington, D.C.: January 31, 2007

Sen. Joseph Biden of Delaware declared himself a candidate for president today, but found the announcement overshadowed by his description of Barack Obama as "the first mainstream African-American who is articulate and bright and clean and a nice-looking guy."

Biden made the comments in an interview with the *New York Observer* published hours before he declared his candidacy. Biden said he meant no insult to the Illinois senator or to other black politicians who might've been slighted by comparison as inarticulate or unclean.

Biden, who was first elected to the Senate in 1972, called Obama "probably the most exciting candidate the Democratic or Republican parties have produced since I've been around. He's fresh, new, smart, insightful. Lightning in a jar."

He added in a conference call: "I really regret some have taken totally out of context my use of the word 'clean.' My mother has a saying, 'clean as a whistle, sharp as a tack.' That is the context. He is crisp and clear."

Biden said he called Obama to assure him he meant no insult.

"I took no offense," Obama said later. "I think Joe was just making news, being Joe. Joe, I think, certainly didn't intend to offend and I'll leave it at that. He called me. He was very gracious and I have no problems with Joe Biden."

Obama added that, although he didn't take Biden's comments personally, his remarks were "historically inaccurate."

"African-American presidential candidates like Jesse Jackson, Shirley Chisholm, Carol Moseley Braun and Al Sharpton gave a voice to many important issues through their campaigns, and no one would call them inarticulate," Obama said.

The statement drowned out Biden's hope to launch his long-shot campaign with a focus on his experience in the Senate and familiarity with foreign policy. It also served as a reminder of his tendency to talk too much and get himself in trouble.

— Steven Thomma and Margaret Talev/ McClatchy Washington Bureau

Obama spent almost 11 months campaigning for president before anyone cast a vote. The effort began in Springfield, Illinois, and ended on the eve of the Iowa caucuses. Here, he addressed supporters in Jefferson, Iowa. (Chuck Kennedy/ MCT)

THE LONG TREK

Setting out

With nod to the 16th president, Obama enters the race

Springfield, Illinois: February 10, 2007

Walking in Lincoln's footsteps, Barack Obama of Illinois today declared his candidacy for the 2008 Democratic presidential nomination. He vowed to change politics and unify a divided people around common goals such as fighting terrorism and expanding health care.

"We can build a more hopeful America," Obama said in front of the former Illinois Capitol. "And that is why, in the shadow of the Old State Capitol, where Lincoln once called on a house divided to stand together, where common hopes and common dreams still live, I stand before you today to announce my candidacy for president of the United States of America."

More than a thousand supporters braved 13-degree cold to cheer him on.

As Obama entered a growing field of candidates eager to lead the post-Bush era, he carried surprising strength for a newcomer to the national stage — but also vulnerabilities that rivals such as Hillary Clinton, John Edwards and Bill Richardson will seek to exploit.

He offers a civil approach to politics that appeals to voters weary of partisan battles in Washington. Unlike rivals, he did not criticize President Bush by name today. Yet the 45-year-old has less experience in national politics than most of the other candidates — just two years so far in the U.S. Senate after seven years in the Illinois Senate. That's one reason he chose to kick off his campaign here — to remind people that Lincoln also had served just two years in Congress and a comparable eight years in the Illinois legislature before winning the White House.

"I know I haven't spent a lot of time learning the ways of Washington," Obama said. "But I've been there long enough to know that the ways of Washington must change."

Obama reminded people that he did have a record in the legislature — working to reform the death penalty, expand health care coverage for children, regulating ethics.

He used the speech to set his campaign's broad themes, insisting that government alone would not solve all problems:

"Each of us, in our own lives, will have to accept

A bundled-up crowd turned out in 13-degree temperatures to hear Obama's announcement, above and facing page. (Zia Nizami/ Belleville News-Democrat)

responsibility for instilling an ethic of achievement in our children, for adapting to a more competitive economy, for strengthening our communities, and sharing some measure of sacrifice."

He argued that a new politics, more than new policies, was needed to fix pressing problems. Obama spoke repeatedly of a new generation, one free of political divisions dating to the 1960s.

"We know the challenges," he said. "What's stopped us from meeting these challenges is not the absence of sound policies and sensible plans. What's stopped us is the failure of leadership, the smallness of our politics — the ease with which we're distracted by the petty and trivial, our chronic avoidance of tough decisions, our preference for scoring cheap political points instead of rolling up our sleeves and building a working consensus to tackle big problems."

Obama wrote the speech himself over the last several days, and rehearsed it with a teleprompter last evening in the basement of the Old State Capitol, according to his spokesman, Robert Gibbs. Gibbs said the ties to Lincoln were deliberate—but not meant to imply that Obama put himself in Lincoln's league.

"This isn't a comparison," Gibbs said. "We're just hoping to borrow a little of that" Lincoln aura.

— *Steven Thomma/ McClatchy Washington Bureau*

Widely considered the leading Democratic candidate in early 2007, Hillary Clinton spoke at a candidate forum on a western campaign tour. (Brian Baer/Sacramento Bee/MCT)

As frontrunner, Clinton stumps the Bay Area

San Francisco: February 23, 2007

Hillary Clinton told a gathering of almost a thousand supporters today that some still questioned whether a woman could be elected president.

"My response to that is, we won't know until we try," Clinton said to loud applause. "Certainly, that's not a hard sell in the home of Nancy Pelosi, Dianne Feinstein and Barbara Boxer," referring to the speaker of the House of Representatives, who's from San Francisco, and California's two senators.

Clinton, the New York senator considered an early front-runner for the Democratic presidential nomination, was on a swing through the Bay Area to raise money for an election that is still a year away.

Those who attended the luncheon at the Sheraton Palace Hotel paid at least $250 for a box lunch including "locally grown sustainable organic produce." Some contributed as much as $4,600, the legal limit for the 2008 primary and general elections.

Clinton talked for more than an hour on a range of subjects, demonstrating the kind of familiarity with policy for which she and her husband have become well-known. Clinton touched on Pell Grants — she wants to increase them and make them year-round — Section 8 housing, and the challenges of remaking the health-care system. Yet as usual in this unusually

early presidential campaign season, the war in Iraq took center stage.

As war protestors chanted and held up signs such as "We Need a Peace President" and "Be a Woman of Peace," Clinton responded, "Yes, we do need to end the war."

She said America's reputation abroad had suffered under President Bush.

"We need a president who will begin to repair the damage, reach out to the rest of the world, who understands that, yes, we may have the strongest military in the world, but the best use of our military is not to use it," she said. "I'd like to see the number of troops capped, which would mean the president couldn't send more there.

"I'd also like to make it against the law for the president to send any young man or woman wearing the uniform of the United States into any war zone without the equipment and the training" necessary to do the job.

She called on Bush to convene an international conference on Iraq and "get over this counterproductive idea that he has that you don't talk to bad people."

She elicited a laugh by adding, "You know, some of us in some of the situations we find ourselves in, wouldn't have anybody to talk to."

-- John Hill/ The Sacramento Bee

South Carolina: 'Let's go to work'

Columbia, South Carolina: February 16, 2007

He fought his way through the crowd, shaking hands and posing for pictures. When he finally reached the square stage reserved for him, Barack Obama took the crowd from jubilant to frenzied.

"How you doing, South Carolina!" he called out. "Look at this! Look at this! Goodness gracious!"

He was off and running, bringing the diverse crowd of 2,800 in the Columbia Metropolitan Convention Center along with him. Obama made his first campaign visit to the state today and promised he'd be back often.

In a 40-minute address from the middle of the room, flanked by two giant American flags and one brilliant blue Palmetto State banner, Obama carried the room through parts of his typical stump speech and moments of inspiration.

Obama responded to criticism from a black state senator who last week endorsed Hillary Clinton for president. Robert Ford of Charleston said Obama couldn't win the White House because he was black, and would drag down the rest of the Democratic ticket if he was nominated. Although he never mentioned Ford, Obama won his biggest cheers of the evening when he responded to the comments.

"Everybody is entitled to their opinion," Obama said, "but I know this: That when folks were saying, 'We're going to march for our freedom,' somebody said, 'You can't do that.' And somebody said, 'Don't sit at the lunch counter, don't share our table.' We can't do that. We can't."

The crowd shouted so loudly that Obama's amplified voice was lost in the response: "Yes we can! Yes we can!"

Much of his address was dedicated to introducing himself to a state that holds a key position in the presidential nomination process with its first-in-the-South Democratic primary on January 29, 2008.

Obama last visited the state in 2004, while he was a member of the Illinois state Senate and a candidate for the U.S. Senate. He returned today as part phenomenon, part unknown, but he has established himself out of the gate as one of the front-runners for the party's nomination.

— By Aaron Gould Sheinin/ The State, Columbia, South Carolina

Texas: Thousands cheer call to end war

Austin, Texas: Feb. 23, 2007

Barack Obama received a rock star's reception today at his first public appearance in Texas since declaring his candidacy. Organizers estimated as many as 20,000 people crowded into an Austin park to hear him rail against the war in Iraq and take subtle digs at his chief rival.

Speaking from an open-air stage in a drizzle, he urged the largely adoring crowd to reject the politics of cynicism and to embrace a message of optimism.

"It is time for us to bring this war to an end," he said, drawing the largest cheer of his 40-minute speech, which was delivered without notes. "We cannot stay the course we are on because it's leading to more death and destruction."

Obama pointed out that even though he was not elected to the Senate until 2004 he had publicly stated his opposition to the congressional resolution in 2002 allowing President Bush to use military force to topple Saddam Hussein. Hillary Clinton voted for the resolution in the Senate, but now says she was misled about the intelligence suggesting Iraq was developing weapons of mass destruction.

The Obama and Clinton camps have traded jabs in recent days after Hollywood mogul David Geffen, one-time supporter of President Clinton, criticized the former first lady as "polarizing." A Clinton aide then suggested that Obama return the $1.3 million he had raised at a Hollywood event hosted by Geffen and apologize for not keeping his pledge to run a campaign free of finger-pointing toward fellow Democrats. Obama's camp quickly returned fire, recalling that Geffen had raised millions for former President Clinton.

In Austin, Obama urged his supporters to make small donations to his campaign and to encourage their friends to follow suit.

"I don't to have to raise all of my money in Hollywood," he said with a smile.

— John Moritz/Fort Worth Star-Telegram

Iraq: Who stood where, when?

Cambridge, Massachusetts: March 19, 2007

A civil discussion this evening at Harvard University about the 2008 presidential campaign broke into a heated confrontation over Iraq between top strategists for Hillary Clinton and Barack Obama.

Clinton adviser Mark Penn lashed out at Obama's claims to be the only candidate who opposed the now-unpopular Iraq war. Penn said Obama once appeared to side with President Bush on the war, then stayed mute on it once he was in the Senate.

Obama strategist David Axelrod criticized Penn's attack as slash-and-burn politics.

"Are we going to spend 10 months savaging each other, or are we going to try to lift this country up?" Axelrod asked.

Occuring as it did in the early weeks of the fast-developing campaign, the clash underscored the high stakes and underlying tensions between the two Democratic camps.

The confrontation came at the end of a 90-minute discussion by managers of three Democratic campaigns in front of students at Harvard's Institute of Politics. The strategist for John Edwards, Jonathan Prince, sat silently between the two others as they squared off.

Penn started it when a student asked him to defend Clinton's 2002 vote to authorize the Iraq war. He repeated Clinton's explanation that she took responsibility for the vote but wouldn't apologize for it because Bush mishandled the authority Congress gave him. Penn said voters should look not at the past but to the future, and how candidates would end the war.

Then he turned on Obama, whose campaign emphasizes that he opposed the war in 2002 while a member of the Illinois Senate. Penn said Obama told reporters at the 2004 Democratic National Convention that there wasn't any difference between him and Bush on the war at that point. He quoted Obama as saying he didn't really know how he would've voted on the 2002 war resolution because he didn't have access to the same intelligence as members of the Senate.

"When he got to the Senate," Penn added, "he didn't give a speech for over a year on Iraq, while Senator Clinton gave six."

Axelrod called that misleading. Obama was the keynote speaker at the 2004 Democratic National Convention. As such, he was pressed to reconcile his opposition to the 2002 war resolution with the yes votes by both Democratic nominees, John Kerry and Edwards.

Axelrod said that Obama put it this way in 2004: "Look, I wasn't in the Senate. I don't know what they were looking at. But what I was looking at told me that this was the wrong war, that it wasn't justified, and that it would lead to a quagmire."

In fact, however, Obama told *The Chicago Tribune* in 2004 that "there's not that much difference between my position and George Bush's position at this stage. The difference, in my mind, is who's in a position to execute."

The two campaign strategists characterized their clash differently. Penn cast it as a choice over the campaigns' focus.

"Is this election going to turn on what happened in 2002 or about the future?" he said.

Axelrod said the argument showed differences of character.

"It is important, if we're going to run the kind of campaign that will lift our party and will move our party forward, that we do it in an honest way," Axelrod said. "That was not an honest way."

— *Steven Thomma/*
McClatchy Washington Bureau

Obama in March 2007. (Chuck Kennedy/MCT)

The question of ethnicity

Oakland, California: April 1, 2007

It was a St. Patrick's Day celebration in this heavily African-American city, and the rally for presidential candidate Barack Obama hopped to a multicultural beat.

A brassy band blared funk tunes as white college kids bared their stomachs, spelling out O-B-A–M–A in fluorescent green body paint. Campaign volunteers in varied ethnic shades donned St. Paddy's Day T-shirts, including one dark-skinned woman swaying in a green top that read, "Kiss me! I'm Kenyan!"

The Obama phenomenon fully bloomed as he took the stage before a cheering throng estimated at 12,000. They packed City Hall Plaza and six blocks of downtown Oakland to see a candidate who is generating crowds in California like no other entrant in the presidential race.

The Illinois senator is a leading anti-war candidate, and a fresh face who says he will renew the spirit of America. But the reason Obama is such a public attraction may well center on one word: race. Some political observers and social scientists say Obama's remarkable drawing power in campaign stops reflects a unique moment in history: He is seen as the first African American with at least a chance to win the White House.

Others say his appeal is fueled by a different racial message. It is that Obama is a mixed-race, multicultural figure who defies ethnic labeling and thus is viewed as a uniting force.

His magnetic lure in public is no guarantee of success in the privacy of America's election booths, where voters' racial hopes or fears can play out in starkly different ways. At his California campaign rallies — and even at stops for other presidential contenders — he provokes a remarkable discussion.

In Oakland, where African-American Mayor Ron Dellums introduced Obama to "the city that has the audacity to welcome the diversity of the world," Jamaican-born Shorron Levy said Obama reflected her own struggles of fitting in.

"Because I'm Jamaican, people say: 'You're not black enough. You haven't had the experience,'" said Levy, director of a Caribbean community Internet television station. "I'm multiracial. I'm black. I'm Jamaican. My father is Jewish. My grandfather is Caucasian. Barack can relate to that. We've experienced the same things."

In Berkeley, an undecided white voter at a campaign speech by John Edwards explained why he may choose Obama.

"With all the issues of race in America, it would be wonderful to have someone of his charisma — and an African-American — as a leader," said Mike Napolitano, an environmental scientist.

If so, it would be a remarkable journey. In Obama's 1995 book, *Dreams from My Father,* he wrote: "I was engaged in a fitful internal struggle. I was trying to raise myself to be a black man in America and, beyond the given of my appearance, no one around me seemed to know exactly what that meant."

Shannon Steen, an assistant professor in American studies and performance arts at the University of California, Berkeley, said it was Obama's triumph over his internal angst that gives him "that magical presence" to connect with people.

"Obama is a really terrific actor, and I mean that in a best sense," said Steen, who is due to deliver a paper, "Barack Obama: Performing Race on the American Political Stage," at Stanford University this month. "People see him as a potential symbol of unity at a time when the country is so divided about so many things."

But Timothy O'Brien, a Los Angeles "personal branding" specialist who coaches executives and public speakers to become "the person to see," said Obama's appeal had nothing to do with multiracialism.

He said Obama was a crowd draw for one reason only — because he is viewed as African American.

"It all begins because he is seen as a candidate who is African-American who has a legitimate shot for the White House," O'Brien said. "People find that intoxicating.

"Al Sharpton wasn't a legitimate candidate for president. Jesse Jackson wasn't a legitimate candidate for president. But Barack Obama is. And he's charismatic — even Kennedyesque."

Among a few African-American intellectuals, that stirs another debate: Is he black enough?

Earlier this year, New York Daily News columnist Stanley Crouch wrote: "When black Americans refer

People of various hues reached for Obama's hand at a rally in Columbia, South Carolina. (C. Aluka Berry/The State, Columbia, South Carolina)

to Obama as 'one of us,' I don't know what they're talking about. He has not lived the life of a black American."

Author Debra J. Dickerson echoed similar issues in a Salon.com story entitled: "Color Blind: Barack Obama would be the great black hope in the next presidential race — if he were actually black."

Rep. Jesse Jackson Jr., an Obama national campaign co-chair, dismisses such debate as "manufactured," saying, "There is a certain absurdity to it."

But Jackson, whose Chicago-area congressional district overlaps with the Illinois state Senate district where Obama served for eight years, recalls how Obama worked to establish himself with Chicago's black residents.

Obama was a community organizer in Chicago and later returned to the city as a civil rights lawyer after becoming the first African-American editor of the *Harvard Law Review*.

Yet in 2000, Obama was routed when he ran for Congress against Rep. Bobby Rush, a former Black Panther who chided Obama as a Harvard and "Hyde Park" elitist out of touch with Chicago's disenfranchised citizens. Now Rush supports Obama for president. And Jackson says the Illinois senator symbolizes a new generation of African-Americans working their way up inside — not outside — the political system.

"I think what is happening in the African-American community is there is a substantial and stylistic transition taking place, and Barack Obama is at the apex of that transition," he said.

On March 4, Obama joined veteran civil rights leaders poignantly crossing the Edmund Pettus Bridge, where in 1965 black marchers were brutally beaten by white Alabama troopers.

"Don't tell me I'm not coming home when I come to Selma, Alabama!" Obama later thundered at an African-American church. He pronounced himself a generational "offspring" of the black struggle for voting rights.

Yet reflecting on his Selma appearance in Oakland, he tailored his remarks differently:

"Some folks thought that celebration was 'a black thing.' I said you don't understand, this is 'an American thing.'"

"I'm endlessly fascinated by the way that he knows he must negotiate a relationship with African American culture and history without claiming it," said Louis Chude-Sokei, a University of California Santa Cruz professor who wrote a book on racial stereotypes among American blacks and African immigrants in early Harlem.

At the Oakland rally, house framer Fred Payne, 48, an African-American, said he was both fascinated and fed up with the talk of race that Obama's candidacy stirred.

Angered by those who would question Obama's racial authenticity, he asked, "Do you have to join a club to be black?"

But he added: "I think Obama is smart enough to realize our environment and race doesn't define us and, as a nation and people, we must recognize that.

"Everybody has rights. Obama knows he has to speak for the rights of everyone."

— *Peter Hecht/ The Sacramento Bee*

The money rolls in

Obama approaches Clinton's fundraising total

Washington, D.C.: April 4, 2007

Barack Obama announced today that his presidential campaign had raised $25 million in the first quarter of 2007. The number grabbed the political world's attention and threatened Hillary Clinton's hope of locking up the Democratic nomination early.

The showing came closer than expected to Clinton's announcement three days ago that she had raised a record $26 million in the same three-month period. Strategists said Obama's total established him as a serious threat to Clinton and signaled the challenges that John Edwards and several other Democrats with less money faced as they competed for the nomination.

"There's not much oxygen left for anyone but the front-runners," said John Lapp, a Democratic strategist who isn't connected with the Obama or Clinton campaigns.

Obama's campaign also reported that his money came from more than 100,000 donors, twice the number that Clinton reported for the first quarter. Half of Obama's donors gave relatively small amounts via the Internet; $6.9 million collectively, or an average of $138 each. An Obama spokeswoman declined to elaborate on the other 50,000 donors, who gave most of the money. Obama has ruled out accepting contributions from political action committees and lobbyists.

Donor contributions are limited by law to $2,300 each for the primary season and the general election.

Clinton's team hasn't said how much of her total is reserved for the general election, but Obama's campaign said all but $1.5 million of the $25 million could go to the primary election.

Edwards is running third in the Democrats' "money primary"; he reported raising $14 million in the year's first quarter.

Obama's announcement came as he campaigned in Iowa, where Steffen Schmidt, a professor of political science at Iowa State University, suggested that "Hillary Clinton's campaign is freaked out" by the news:

"They're going, 'What's happening? Why are all these Democrats abandoning the Clinton juggernaut?'

"Hillary Clinton has been a household word for eight years in the White House and six years in the Senate," Schmidt said, "and Barack Obama came from essentially sort of nowhere. It is very dangerous for Hillary Clinton because . . . there are lots of people in the Democratic Party saying Hillary Clinton is not electable, is divisive, that you don't know who the real Hillary Clinton is."

— *Margaret Talev/*
McClatchy Washington Bureau

Obama close to Clinton

Barack Obama rivals Hillary Clinton's record. What 2008 presidential candidates raised in the first three months of 2007, in millions:

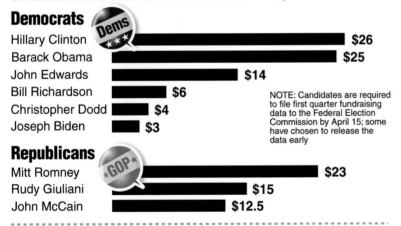

Democrats

Hillary Clinton	$26
Barack Obama	$25
John Edwards	$14
Bill Richardson	$6
Christopher Dodd	$4
Joseph Biden	$3

NOTE: Candidates are required to file first quarter fundraising data to the Federal Election Commission by April 15; some have chosen to release the data early

Republicans

Mitt Romney	$23
Rudy Giuliani	$15
John McCain	$12.5

Previous records

For the first quarter of the year before a presidential election

Dems Al Gore, 1999	**$8.9**
GOPs Phil Gramm, 1995	**$8.7**

• George W. Bush, in his first full quarter of presidential campaign fundraising, April-June 1999, raised $29 million

Democrats begin a string of debates

Democratic presidential candidates lined up on stage in South Carolina. (Gerry Melendez/The State, Columbia, South Carolina)

Orangeburg, South Carolina: April 26, 2007

Candidates for the 2008 Democratic presidential nomination eyed each other politely — even warily — tonight in their first face-to-face debate. The eight candidates differed sharply with President Bush, particularly on Iraq, but seldom with one another. The format did not allow them to directly challenge each other — and few did.

Rather, they mostly agreed in their desire to get U.S. troops out of Iraq, to expand health care to the uninsured while controlling costs for those with insurance, to support abortion rights without qualification, and to bar access to guns for the mentally ill like the gunman who killed 32 at Virginia Tech.

Absent direct challenges — or any pronounced gaffes — the debate probably did nothing to fundamentally change the shape of the contest with Hillary Clinton, Barack Obama and John Edwards leading in the polls and the rest trailing well behind.

Mark Penn, senior strategist to the Clinton campaign, said it was too early to expect direct attacks that would turn off voters just getting to know the candidates.

Sponsored by the South Carolina Democratic Party, the 90-minute debate was moderated by NBC newsman Brian Williams on the campus of South Carolina State University.

There were a couple of light spots in the evening.

One came from little-known Mike Gravel, a former senator from Alaska, when he was asked to explain his presence in the campaign and the debate.

"Some of these people frighten me," Gravel said, to laughter.

The other moment belonged to Joseph Biden. Asked by Williams whether he could control his exceedingly verbose style on the world stage, Biden gave a one-word answer: "Yes."

— Steven Thomma/
McClatchy Washington Bureau

Preston Simmons, left, and Trovious Starr, right, cheered for Obama in front of South Carolina State University's main entrance in Orangeburg (Gerry Melendez/The State, Columbia, South Carolina)

Learning the ropes

Poor showing helped Obama adapt his approach to unions

Washington, D.C.: May 14, 2007

Barack Obama is going to school on the presidential campaign trail, and he just got a lesson from what's arguably the most important union in Democratic Party politics. Obama got poor marks from the International Association of Firefighters for a speech he gave in March courting union support. Worse, the union gave several rivals, including Hillary Clinton, much better grades.

The problem, union President Harold Schaitberger said in an interview, was that Obama all but ignored the union issues that firefighters cared about. His lofty speech seemed aimed more at the C-SPAN audience outside the Capitol Hill ballroom.

"There was a view that Senator Obama seemed to be a little somber, a little sobering," Schaitberger said, referring to a survey he took of the roughly 1,000 union leaders who heard Obama and 10 other candidates that day. "The issues he shared weren't necessarily on point.

"Senator Obama was probably not overly pleased with my opinion," Schaitberger added. "But I was being honest."

By comparison, Clinton punctuated her speech with repeated references not only to her personal connection to firefighters in New York but also to her support for issues they cared deeply about, such as health care for those hurt or made ill by work at the World Trade Center site or better radio and search gear to help guide them through another disaster.

Firefighters also thought highly of Joseph Biden and Christopher Dodd, John Edwards and Bill Richardson.

"All five of them did a terrific job," Schaitberger said.

Today, Obama got a chance for a makeover. The firefighters invited him and the five Democrats who did well to meet for follow-up interviews with about 80 union leaders gathered in Portsmouth, New Hampshire.

Obama literally phoned it in, from a campaign stop in Iowa, but he acknowledged the faux pas and blamed his staff for not scheduling him to be there in person. Then he got more specific about firefighter issues and ended up with a much better grade.

"He was more on point," Schaitberger said. "He acknowledged this. He made it clear that he really wanted to pursue our support. Today was a very different presentation."

Democratic candidates are courting lots of unions, including such big ones as the 1.4-million-member American Federation of State, County and Municipal Employees and the 1.8-million-member Service Employees International Union. Yet the 280,000-member firefighters union might be even more powerful in Democratic caucuses and primaries. One major reason: They're everywhere there's a firehouse. Another: They're popular, especially since Sept. 11.

— Steven Thomma/
McClatchy Washington Bureau

Mixing with the crowd at a southern feast

Obama at South Carolina Rep. Jim Clyburn's fish fry in Columbia, South Carolina on April 27, 2007. (Gary O'Brien/Charlotte Observer/MCT)

Flooded with funds

Washington, D.C.: July 1, 2007

Barack Obama has raised more in a three-month period than any other Democratic presidential contender in history, his campaign said today, giving the freshman senator a symbolic boost and $32.5 million as he chases Hillary Clinton's lead in national polls.

The third-place Democrat, John Edwards, had to make do with $9 million for the second quarter of the year, which just ended. That met Edwards' announced goal but represented only a third of the $27 million Clinton's campaign estimated it would report for the same period, and compared more closely with the $7 million announced by distant fourth-place Democrat Bill Richardson.

Obama's camp was overjoyed with its second-quarter results. Besides the money — $31 million of which can be spent on the primary election contest alone — the campaign reported another record of 258,000 donors.

Campaign manager David Plouffe wrote in a memo to supporters that the fundraising so far had greatly surpassed the Obama team's own expectations and would allow Obama to keep up with former first lady Clinton.

"When we entered this race, we did not think that was possible," Plouffe wrote.

Tops in campaign cash '08

What the top three 2008 presidential candidates raised in the first two quarters of 2007, in millions:

Democrats	1st qtr.	2nd qtr.	To date
Barack Obama	$25.6	$32.5	$58.1
Hillary Clinton	$26.0	$27.0	$53.0
John Edwards	$14.0	$9.0	$23.0

• Obama had the most donors; 258,000 so far this year

Republicans	1st qtr.	2nd qtr.	To date
Mitt Romney	$23.4	$20.5	$43.9
Rudy Giuliani	$16.0	$17.0	$33.0
John McCain	$13.6	$11.2	$24.8

• Romney has given $9 million in personal loans to his campaign

© 2007 MCT   Source: McClatchy Washington Bureau   Graphic: Melina Yingling, Judy Treible

"We estimated at this point of the campaign we'd be at least $20 (million) - 25 million behind one of our fellow candidates. Remarkably, we should be on at least even financial footing for the duration of the campaign."

— *Margaret Talev with Steven Thomma/ McClatchy Washington Bureau*

Iowans heard Obama ask them to take a leap of faith and join his campaign. Already the money was taking the leap, putting Obama in first place in fund-raising by the middle of 2007. (James Colburn/ MCT)

Obama joked with his secret service staff before a campaign rally at the Fort Worth Convention Center. (Tom Pennington/Fort Worth Star-Telegram/MCT)

Secret Service protects Obama early

Washington, D.C.: July 2, 2007

The U.S. Secret Service, which faces a big-time security strain as the 2008 presidential campaign heats up, already is spending $44,000 a day on around-the-clock security for Sen. Barack Obama.

Obama, who has talked openly about the possibility of getting shot, is the first of 18 presidential candidates to be assigned a security detail. Hillary Clinton is the only other candidate who's getting protection, qualifying as a former first lady.

Obama has been assigned a security detail since May 3, more than eight months before the first votes will be cast in the Iowa caucuses. That's the earliest a presidential candidate has ever qualified for protection.

Major presidential candidates and their spouses generally do not qualify for protection until 120 days before a general election, but there have been exceptions. The Rev. Jesse Jackson, a Democrat, got protection in 1984 and 1988 after receiving threats during his presidential runs. Decisions to provide early protection are made by a special five-member committee, made up of top House and Senate leaders of both parties.

The Secret Service won't say what prompted the decision to protect Obama at such an early date. The first-term senator has drawn particularly large crowds on the campaign trail this year.

Overall, the Secret Service wants to spend more than $100 million on campaign protection in 2008, roughly $35 million more than it spent in 2004.

The Secret Service protects the president and vice president, their families, former presidents, visiting foreign heads of state and government and major presidential and vice presidential candidates and their spouses. In addition, the agency will take the lead in securing the national political conventions in Denver and Minneapolis-St. Paul next year.

— *Rob Hotakainen/Sacramento Bee,*
San Luis Obispo Tribune

How he connects

Running first in fundraising and second nationally among Democratic presidential contenders, Barack Obama is asking voters to take a leap of faith and embrace the promise of his charismatic leadership to change America.

He's betting that voters will rally behind his motivational style and personal appeal despite his relatively thin national credentials, that they'll choose him as a clean slate for the future rather than restore a Clinton political dynasty and that they'll embrace his idealistic if vague vision of a unified, post-racial America.

"There is this narrow window that doesn't come around that often — maybe once a generation — where we have the opportunity to put our shoulder into the wheel and move history in a better direction," Obama told about 1,000 people who were gathered around a gazebo in the old-fashioned town square in Fairfield, Iowa. There, residents are known for their interests in meditation and environmental consciousness.

"That's the moment we're in," Obama exhorted, his voice building steam. "But we've got to seize it."

In any setting, Obama seems to relish the moments after a speech, when adults and children swarm to shake his hand...

"If we seize it together," he said, allowing the last word to linger, "we are going to transform the United States of America. It's a matter of who can ignite the American people to build a movement for change."

That's the soul of Obama's message. Many Democrats find it electrifying. In campaign stops during a two-day swing through southeast Iowa last week, the Illinois senator didn't try to compete with the strengths of his two main rivals who led him in polls here, the first state to vote in next year's nomination contests.

Obama's depth of experience is no match for Hillary Clinton's years of national political training. Nor can he equal the amount of time that John Edwards already has invested in cultivating Iowa Democrats. Edwards has all but lived here for 18 months.

Even Obama's policy applause lines aren't much different from theirs: Get U.S. troops out of Iraq, expand health-care coverage, mandate more fuel-efficient cars.

But he uses "shoulder to the wheel" imagery at nearly every stop. He speaks of a "politics of hope," a "hunger" for change and a philosophy that individual fates are interconnected, "that I am my brother's keeper, my sister's keeper."

And when this African-American speaks of his implicit promise to lead America beyond race, his cues are evocative but indirect. He talks of America having survived harder times, and of moving past eras of war, slavery, segregation, even the civil rights movement.

In a brief interview, weaving past fans at a July Fourth baseball game in Des Moines, Obama acknowledged the racial subtext of his stump speech:

"I think that's one division that needs to be bridged. But it's one of many. I also think I've got the capacity to build bridges between Republicans and Democrats, the division between the secular and the religious."

The voters who came to see Obama — at an elementary school in Keokuk, a coffeehouse in Oskaloosa, a backyard in Pella, a July Fourth picnic in a Des Moines park — covered the spectrum: Democrats, independents, past Bush supporters who regret the war. Most were white.

In any setting, Obama seems to relish the moments after a speech, when adults and children swarm to shake his hand, have a photo snapped or collect an autograph. Some just want to confide in him.

In one receiving line at a backyard gathering in Mount Pleasant, Eleanor Longfield, a modest, gray-haired woman, told Obama that her 37-year-old son, an Army major with three children, was about to be deployed to Iraq for a third time. She was scared. Obama placed both hands on the retired nurse's shoulders. He held her gaze and told her he wants to bring the troops home. "I'll pray for you," he said. As tears welled in her eyes, he hugged her close.

Shaking, Longfield ducked out to compose herself. She headed to a table of lemonade and cookies under a shade tree.

"It's between Obama and Edwards," she said, "but after today I'm leaning toward Obama."

Obama's energy feeds off the crowds. Before small audiences, he sometimes comes across as professorial, his words and gestures measured. The bigger the audience, the louder and more instinctive his speech becomes. His tall, slim frame exudes new energy. At

Obama spoke at a campaign stop outside the home of Dan and Heather Vroom in Pella, Iowa, July 4, 2007 (James Colburn/MCT)

a small event, he said cars should be getting 45 miles a gallon. Hours later, he told a much larger crowd he could see cars soon getting 50 mpg — even 60!

He also can be disarmingly goofy.

In the middle of one speech outdoors, he started coughing uncontrollably, then admitted, laughing, that he'd just swallowed a gnat. He tried to continue but the coughing overtook him.

"Don't film that!' he pleaded to a camera crew, as the audience chuckled. "That's all right. I hadn't had lunch yet — protein." An aide brought him a drink and he picked up where he left off.

Verona Williams, 70, a black, retired after-school teacher, brought her 11-year-old grandson, Noah, to get an autograph at a Keokuk event in an elementary school. She also brought an old cowbell she'd bought at an auction.

"Hearing his speech, I had to ring the bell for him," she explained. "The children of all races will see how united the United States has become. That's going to be a start."

Many expect their decisions to come down to Clinton or Obama.

Fairfield Mayor Ed Malloy met Clinton years ago and considers her most qualified. He met Obama last week for the first time.

"I like Hillary Clinton, but I still have to get over some of the votes she made on the war," Malloy said.

With Obama, Malloy said, "I came away very, very impressed. I think he's got a natural capacity to inspire. On an inspiration, gut feeling right now, I'd say I'm closer to Senator Obama."

— *Margaret Talev/*
McClatchy Washington Bureau

Michelle Obama builds him up — and keeps him grounded

Michelle Obama took the microphone at an Iowa campaign stop in July 2007. (James Colburn/MCT)

Oskaloosa, Iowa: July 6, 2007

"The question isn't whether he's ready."

It was midmorning on the Fourth of July when Michelle Obama issued this rhetorical challenge to a few hundred Iowans crammed inside the retro-modern, brick-and-loft Smokey Row coffeehouse.

"Because he's ready," she said. "It's whether we're ready. He is the real thing. Are we ready for that? Together we can turn the page; we can move into the next phase of what this country can be."

Since Barack Obama formally announced his campaign for the Democratic nomination five months ago, Michelle Obama is still testing the limits of her complex public role as her husband's biggest champion, corporate supermom-on-leave and taskmaster who sometimes cuts the candidate down to size and keeps him grounded.

She's not like other candidates' wives; she's a tall, striking, tell-it-like-it-is black woman from modest roots, with a Harvard law degree and a career as a hospital executive that's on hold for now.

They met when she was assigned to guide him through a summer job at a law firm.

She and the couple's girls — Malia, who celebrated her ninth birthday on the road last week, and Sasha, 6 — aren't staples on the campaign trail, but they sometimes function as closers of sorts in occasional appearances.

Barack Obama lets Sasha, a ball of energy, swing on his arms at events. He also helped a crowd sing "Happy Birthday" to the more reserved Malia. He announced at one stop that he'd bested one of the girls at a card game of UNO.

And he shows his wife a good dose of respect.

"I'm going to record all this," he told one crowd, after Michelle Obama had built him up, "so when I do something boneheaded at home — forget to take out the garbage — I can say, 'See, honey? I'm the real deal.'"

Obama, an on-again-off-again cigarette smoker for years, was cowed into quitting largely by his wife, who told him he could smoke or run for president, but he couldn't do both, according to a campaign aide who asked not to be named to avoid annoying his bosses. The aide said that Obama kept nicotine gum on hand.

At the coffeehouse, perched in front of the soda counter and dressed in summery outfits, the Obama women established the candidate's place in a warm, close, modern family whose members are willing to sacrifice some of their individual goals — but not all — to support his bid.

"Actually, the campaign wanted us to join them yesterday instead of just today," Michelle Obama told the crowd before introducing her husband. "So I sat the kids down and I said, 'Look, they want us to come out on Tuesday as well.'

"Well, the two of them promptly pulled out their camp calendar, looked it over seriously over the kitchen table, and said, 'Well, Tuesday is the haunted trails trip, so we won't be going to Iowa.'"

The audience laughed and applauded.

"We are doing fine as a family," she told the crowd. "That's one of the things that people want to know most from me as the wife of the candidate: How are we holding up? We're doing our best to keep our kids first. Our view is that if our children aren't sane and whole and focused, then we can't represent that to the rest of the country."

Later, a handler took the girls to play in a nearby park and pet a puppy while their mom worked the coffeehouse with handshakes, hugs and autographs.

"She matters to me very much," said Lesa Nuri, 53,

Michelle Obama with daughters Malia, left, and Sasha. (James Colburn/ MCT)

an office manager at a restaurant, who has children and no health insurance. "Mrs. Obama and the senator are real people."

Barack Obama tells crowds that his wife is "too smart to run for president," a laugh line she tolerates because of what he says next: "She would rather tell the president what to do."

-- Margaret Talev/McClatchy Washington Bureau

YouTube debate puts 'real people' in spotlight

Charleston, South Carolina: July 23, 2007

Sometimes, the questions get as much attention as the answers.

That was the case in 1984 when a reporter asked candidate Gary Hart whether he had cheated on his wife. That was the case as well when a debate questioner in 1988 asked Michael Dukakis how he'd respond if his wife were raped and murdered.

So it was again tonight, as Democratic presidential candidates met at The Citadel college campus to debate. This time, however, they faced questions not from journalists but from voters, whose inquiries were sent in by video via the YouTube Web site.

The questions ran the gamut from serious to offbeat, all in the more familiar voices of real people who put their faces on issues of the day. They included a gay couple asking whether they could be married, a father of a dead soldier asking whether the candidates had family members serving in uniform, and two people who asked pointed questions on Iraq from very different viewpoints.

In one personal video, the Rev. Reggie Longcrier of Hickory, North Carolina, noted that politicians once used religion to justify slavery, segregation and men-only voting.

"So why is it still acceptable to use religion to deny gay Americans their full and equal rights?" he said, pressing John Edwards to justify using his own religious beliefs in explaining his opposition to gay marriage. The normally smooth-talking Edwards appeared to struggle with the question, saying he didn't think a president should impose his religious beliefs on the country — but that he still opposed gay marriage.

In another video, two women identified as Mary and Jen from New York asked, "Would you allow us to be married to each other?"

For the record, Christopher Dodd and Bill Richardson said no; Dennis Kucinich said yes.

There were lighthearted approaches to the videos as well, such as one question posed by a snowman about global warming and another asking whether any of the candidates would serve as president for the minimum wage.

Those who committed to working for minimum wage: Hillary Clinton, Edwards, Mike Gravel, Kucinich and Richardson. Dodd said he couldn't afford to, and Barack Obama said he could afford to work for the minimum wage but didn't commit.

The video questions were culled by CNN from roughly 3,000 sent in via YouTube, which draws hundreds of thousands of video contributions every day.

The march of citizen video into politics might not have the revolutionary impact that television had a half-century ago — despite predictions of such an upheaval today from YouTube's founders. Debates for years have featured questions posed by voters, albeit not with the pizzazz of YouTube.

Still, the role of citizen-generated video and viral marketing via the Internet are already changing politics, at least around the edges, as voters gain a new, less filtered voice and politicians rush to find new ways to reach them.

YouTube's founders and executives said they hoped the video phenomenon would draw more people into politics.

"We saw what TV did for bringing politicians into people's living rooms," said Steve Grove, the head of news and politics for YouTube. "What YouTube is doing now is bringing the voters out of their living rooms."

"It's breaking down barriers," YouTube co-founder Steve Chen said during a lunch with reporters. "You don't have to be in Iowa or New Hampshire to pose a question of the candidates."

It's also changing the way political campaigns pitch those voters.

Just since March, candidates have contributed 1,200 videos, viewed a total of 13 million times. The candidates also unveiled 30-second videos during today's debate, many of them offbeat.

Edwards, for example, juxtaposed pictures of war and poverty with music punctuating what he considers silly criticism of his own expensive haircuts.

"What really matters?" the spot asked.

Dodd tied his white hair with valuable experience, closing with the slogan, "Dodd, the guy with white hair for the White House."

— *Steven Thomma/*
McClatchy Washington Bureau

Obama greeted other candidates before the start of the CNN/Youtube debate.
(Randall Hill/Myrtle Beach Sun-News)

No preconditions: Was that reply naive?

Clinton and Obama during YouTube debate; afterward her campaign skewered his remark about meeting with certain foreign leaders. (Gerry Melendez/The State, Columbia, South Carolina)

Washington, D.C.: July 24, 2007

Hillary Clinton has seized on Barack Obama's debate assertion that he would meet with Cuban leader Fidel Castro and Venezuelan President Hugo Chavez as evidence that her top rival isn't ready for the diplomatic stage.

In one of the sharpest exchanges of the Democratic primary campaign to date, the two camps fired off dueling memos today. Obama's campaign suggested that Clinton had backtracked and the Illinois senator was offering a distinct departure from the Bush administration's refusal to engage in diplomacy.

In Monday night's YouTube debate, the candidates were asked whether they would be willing to meet separately, without preconditions, during the first year of their administrations with leaders of Iran, Syria, Venezuela, Cuba and North Korea.

"I would," Obama said. "The notion that somehow not talking to countries is punishment to them, which has been the guiding diplomatic principle of this administration, is ridiculous."

Clinton, in an Iowa newspaper interview after the debate, called Obama's suggestion of a dialogue with a dictator "irresponsible and frankly naive."

Her campaign also dispatched former Clinton Secretary of State Madeline Albright, who said in a conference call that the New York senator had struck the proper diplomatic tone, ruling out engagement until lower-level talks had been completed.

The back and forth came as front-runner Clinton sought to position herself as best experienced to assume the presidential helm and Obama looked to present himself as a fresh alternative.

"What she's somehow maintaining is my statement could be construed as not having asked what the meeting was about," Obama told Iowa's *Quad City Times*. "I didn't say these guys were going to come over for a cup of coffee some afternoon."

The Clinton campaign issued a memo that suggested he had "committed to presidential-level meetings with some of the world's worst dictators without precondition during his first year in office."

He countered with a statement from Anthony Lake, former President Clinton's national security adviser, who said a "great nation and its president should never fear negotiating with anyone."

"After seven years of arrogant refusal to get into direct bargaining with others," Lake said, "surely it's time for some fresh thinking."

— *Lesley Clark/Miami Herald, Bradenton Herald*

Quick debate exchanges differ from governing

Washington, D.C.: July 30, 2007

As political debates go, it was fine drama when Barack Obama said last week that he'd meet with dictators without preconditions. Hillary Clinton pounced quickly to say that she'd never give some thug like Fidel Castro an open-ended opportunity to score points at the expense of the U.S. president.

The immediate score: a gaffe for Obama and a win for Clinton. It was another sign of how Clinton is a better debater than her younger rival. She's quicker on her feet, more agile, readier with a sound bite that fits a long-range political strategy. Through four debates, it's clear she's better at this test than Obama is.

But that doesn't necessarily mean she'd be the better president. In fact, the debates don't really signal how either one would make decisions in the Oval Office.

Presidents rarely, if ever, have to act alone or in 30-second sound bites, as they do on the debate stage. Even in wartime, presidents get more time and much more opportunity to think through their decisions.

"If there were a nuclear attack, that would be one thing," said presidential historian Robert Dallek. "But that doesn't happen. When there is any military action, it's invariably the consequence of many hours of deliberation."

Consider the most dangerous confrontation of modern times, when President Kennedy risked nuclear war in a 1962 showdown to get the Soviet Union to withdraw missiles from Cuba. The relatively inexperienced Kennedy spent hours and hours working through the crisis with his military and diplomatic advisers, challenging a Pentagon recommendation of airstrikes before settling on the idea of a naval blockade of Cuba.

"They spent 13 days struggling with that," Dallek said.

It was a shining example of presidential leadership and executive management, and none of it came quickly, easily or in a sound bite. History suggests that once in the Oval Office, judgment counts more than the speed and rhetorical agility of debates.

What they said in last week's Democratic debate:

QUESTION: In 1982, Anwar Sadat traveled to Israel, a trip that resulted in a peace agreement that has lasted ever since. In the spirit of that type of bold leadership, would you be willing to meet separately, without precondition, during the first year of your administration, in Washington or anywhere else, with the leaders of Iran, Syria, Venezuela, Cuba and North Korea, in order to bridge the gap that divides our countries?

OBAMA: I would. And the reason is this, that the notion that somehow not talking to countries is punishment to them, which has been the guiding diplomatic principle of this administration — is ridiculous.

Now, Ronald Reagan and Democratic presidents like JFK constantly spoke to the Soviet Union at a time when Ronald Reagan called them an evil empire. And the reason is because they understood that we may not trust them and they may pose an extraordinary danger to this country, but we had the obligation to find areas where we can potentially move forward.

And I think that it is a disgrace that we have not spoken to them. We've been talking about Iraq — one of the first things that I would do in terms of moving a diplomatic effort in the region forward is to send a signal that we need to talk to Iran and Syria because they're going to have responsibilities if Iraq collapses.

They have been acting irresponsibly up until this point. But if we tell them that we are not going to be a permanent occupying force, we are in a position to say that they are going to have to carry some weight, in terms of stabilizing the region.

CLINTON: Well, I will not promise to meet with the leaders of these countries during my first year. I will promise a very vigorous diplomatic effort because I think it is not that you promise a meeting at that high a level before you know what the intentions are.

I don't want to be used for propaganda purposes. I don't want to make a situation even worse. But I certainly agree that we need to get back to diplomacy, which has been turned into a bad word by this administration.

And I will pursue very vigorous diplomacy.

And I will use a lot of high-level presidential envoys to test the waters, to feel the way. But certainly, we're not going to just have our president meet with Fidel Castro and Hugo Chavez and, you know, the president of North Korea, Iran and Syria until we know better what the way forward would be.

— Steven Thomma/
McClatchy Washington Bureau

Obama 'black enough'?

Obama answered questions from members of the National Association of Black Journalists at the group's convention. Next to him was moderator Byron Pitts. (Jae C. Hong/Associated Press)

Las Vegas, Nevada: August 10, 2007

With puzzlement and a touch of humor, Barack Obama weighed in today on a question posed by some in the African-American community about whether he's "black enough" to represent them in the White House.

Speaking to a packed ballroom at the National Association of Black Journalists convention here, Obama said he found the question curious because it appeared to go deeper than his brown skin or his record as a U.S. senator from Illinois or a member of that state's legislature.

"It's not my track record," he told the audience. "It's not that I can't give a pretty good speech; from what I've heard I can preach once in a while. What it really does lay bare, I think, in part: We're still locked into the notion that somehow if you appeal to white folks then there must be something wrong."

Some blacks have questioned his ethnicity because he was raised by a white American mother and an African father, who left the household when Obama was young.

Obama added that his educational background — he attended Harvard Law School — might contribute to some people doubting his racial pedigree.

"There's some of that 'Is he keeping it real because he went to Harvard?' which a lot of you in the audience had to deal with ... you'd think that we'd be over that by now," he said.

He used elements from the old joke about time and so-called "colored people time" as the reason that he was late for convention events.

"You guys keep asking if I'm black enough," he said with a straight face. "I thought I'd just stroll in."

— *William Douglas/*
McClatchy Washington Bureau

In Republican ranks, disarray

Fred Thompson   *John McCain*   *Rudy Giuliani*   *Mike Huckabee*   *Mitt Romney*

Kansas City, Missouri: September 2, 2007

In more than a half-century of watching Republican politics, Hillard Selck has witnessed his share of presidential races. But the one-time Missouri GOP chairman, now 81, says the 2008 version features a distressing twist.

"Confusion. Utter confusion," Selck said of the way many Republicans are sizing up the field.

Labor Day weekend is a traditional time for political appraisal. This year's view of the coming presidential race is especially sobering for Republicans who are struggling to sort through a jumble that offers no consensus front-runner.

One issue: Rudy Giuliani, the former New York City mayor who became a hero to many after the September 11 terrorist attacks, may hold big leads in national polls, but he trails in Iowa and New Hampshire, states that hold the first two big tests. Rival Mitt Romney, who is focusing heavily on the two early states, leads by sizable margins in both and could use wins there to slingshot his way to the front.

And both, Republican insiders moan, must confront their own electoral demons. The twice-divorced Giuliani favors abortion rights and a host of other issues that run counter to the deeply held beliefs of GOP conservatives. Romney has switched stands on abortion in recent years, and his Mormon faith raises questions for some.

"They can't find the crown prince they always look for," said University of Virginia political scientist Larry Sabato.

Fred Thompson, who will officially enter the race

soon, has drawbacks, too. His late entry suggests he and his supporters consider the field suspect.

And John McCain isn't the front-runner he used to be.

Throw in an unpopular war and President Bush's shaky poll numbers and no wonder some Republicans are fretting.

"These are tough times, no question," said longtime Iowa GOP national committeeman Steve Roberts. "You've got the Democrats sensing that 2008 could be a great year for them from the presidency on down, and we've got challenges."

Hillary Clinton, who ranks as the clear Democratic front-runner, and her battle against Barack Obama has sucked away most of the media attention, making it harder for Republican candidates to introduce themselves to a national audience, said GOP pollster Neil Newhouse.

"They've dominated the news and the attention of the voters," he said.

The GOP has avoided unrest in part because the party has a tradition of going with front-runners who run as establishment candidates. Ronald Reagan in 1980. George H.W. Bush in 1988. Bob Dole in 1996. George W. Bush, heir to a political legacy, in 2000.

"We have typically gone with the person whose turn it is," said Tom Rath, a nationally known New Hampshire political strategist who is helping Mitt Romney this year. "One reason there is this undercurrent this year is because we're not used to a race that is genuinely this wide open."

— Steve Kraske/The Kansas City Star

Photos by (from left): *Michael Hickey, Kristin Goode, Erik Campos, John D. Simmons, Chuck Kennedy/MCT.*

Iraq

Obama calls for pulling combat troops by end of '08

Clinton, Iowa: September 12, 2007

Barack Obama unveiled a new, comprehensive plan for Iraq today that features a call to pull out all U.S. combat troops by the end of 2008. Obama sought to position himself in the hearts and minds of Iowa Democrats as the leading get-out-of-Iraq-fast candidate for the presidential nomination. The speech was also an effort to rebut critiques that he doesn't have the experience or policy gravitas of his chief rival, Hillary Clinton.

The junior senator from Illinois unveiled his plan at Ashford University here, in the state where the first votes to choose party presidential nominees will be cast in four months. End-the-war sentiments are strong among Iowa Democrats.

His new plan features four key points:

• Pull out U.S. combat troops immediately at a pace of one to two brigades a month, to be completed by the end of 2008.

• Organize a new constitutional convention in Iraq through the United Nations, and don't let it adjourn until Iraqi leaders reach an accord on reconciliation. Obama said he wouldn't force Iraq to partition itself into Sunni Muslim Arab, Shiite Muslim and Kurdish regions. "It must be their choice."

• Step up diplomacy with all nations in the region to forge a new regional security compact.

• Take immediate steps to relieve the humanitarian disaster in Iraq, including allowing more Iraqi refugees into the U.S.

While the potential appeal of his plan to anti-war Democrats is obvious, the practical impediments to implementing it may be less so.

For starters, Obama isn't president, Bush is, so it won't happen by the end of 2008. Second, military experts say that removing the massive U.S. presence from Iraq that fast may be logistically impossible. Third, Iraq is a sovereign nation and its leaders may object to a would-be American president ordering them to write another constitution. Fourth, seeking a diplomatic security compact doesn't guarantee that regional powers will accept one.

Obama's plan isn't much different from that

Obama listened to Army General David Petraeus testify to the Senate Foreign Relations Committee on the state of the war in Iraq, September 11, 2007. (Chuck Kennedy/ MCT)

of John Edwards, who has called for immediately withdrawing up to 50,000 troops and pulling out all combat troops in about a year. He'd retain U.S. troops in the region to help contain instability and would pursue diplomacy energetically.

Clinton's plan is more measured. She has called for revoking Bush's authority to wage the war, capping U.S. troops in Iraq at January 1 levels and requiring that withdrawal begin within 90 days of that legislation passing. She's also said that, if elected, she would begin withdrawing troops within two months. She has rejected a complete withdrawal, saying that some American troops must stay in Iraq to train Iraqi forces, fight terrorists and protect U.S. interests.

— Margaret Talev/McClatchy Washington Bureau

With clock ticking in Iowa, Obama still trailing

Maquoketa, Iowa: September 13, 2007

Oprah's pulling for him now, he's raking in historic levels of campaign cash and his fans still freak out as if they'd just seen Elvis. But Barack Obama has a potential problem now that Labor Day has come and gone.

He has been stuck about 20 points behind front-runner Hillary Clinton in national polls and appears to be lagging even in South Carolina, a key early primary state, despite its large proportion of black voters, whom he's counting on there.

So he spent two days this week in Iowa angling to reduce the gap. Iowa's caucuses four months from now make it the first state to choose party presidential nominees. Polls there show Obama within five points of Clinton and within three of John Edwards, a frequent visitor since his 2004 run.

"I know that many of you are still shopping for a candidate," Obama told about 300 residents of Maquoketa, population 6,100, who gathered at a park on Thursday morning to hear him. "But it's September now. You can feel that little chill in the air. It's time for us to really make some decisions."

— Margaret Talev/
McClatchy Washington Bureau

Taxes: A plan to overhaul the code

Washington, D.C.: September 18, 2007

Barack Obama proposed a tax overhaul today that could save lower- and middle-class workers and seniors $500 to $1,500 a year by shifting more of the burden to well-off investors and corporations.

His proposed tax cuts and credits, which are aimed at workers earning $50,000 or less per year, would cost the Treasury an estimated $85 billion annually. To offset that loss, the Illinois Democrat said he'd raise the top bracket of tax rates on dividends and capital gains from 15 percent now to as high as 28 percent — where they were in the 1980s under President Reagan.

He also promised to close the "carried-interest" tax loophole, which hedge funds have exploited, to repeal or rein in oil and gas industry breaks and international tax deferrals, and to pressure several countries to stop shielding U.S. tax evaders.

"We've gone too far from being a country where we're all in this together to a country where everyone's on their own," Obama told the Tax Policy Center, a joint project of the Brookings Institution and the Urban Institute, center-left think tanks.

Obama criticized the Bush administration for carving out too many perks for the wealthiest Americans and for companies that, despite those favors, sent jobs and profits overseas. Too much strain on the middle class, he said, ultimately would hurt American competitiveness.

Obama's plan would offset payroll taxes on lower- and middle-class workers with income tax cuts of up to $500 per worker or $1,000 per family. That could eliminate income taxes for 10 million Americans. He also proposed a tax credit of roughly $500 a year for an estimated 10 million middle-class homeowners who don't get the mortgage interest deduction because they don't itemize.

Americans 65 and older who earn less than $50,000 per year wouldn't have to pay federal income tax or even file a return. That would take about 7 million seniors off the income tax rolls — saving each

> "We've gone too far from being a country where we're all in this together to a country where everyone's on their own,"

about $1,400 per year — and save perhaps 22 million seniors from filing income tax returns.

Finally, Obama proposed simplifying tax filings for about 40 million middle-class filers who take the standard deduction. He'd have the Internal Revenue Service send them prepared tax forms based on wage and bank account statements that the government collects. Those filers could simply sign those forms and send them back.

— Margaret Talev/
McClatchy Washington Bureau

Now it's autumn. Who'll overtake Clinton?

Indianola, Iowa: September 21, 2007

Democrats enter the fall campaign with one question hanging over their party: Can anyone catch Hillary Clinton?

The New York senator has combined the party's most popular brand name with a muscular, disciplined campaign to take a commanding position almost everywhere. She has opened double-digit leads over her nearest rivals in national polls, as well as in early voting states such as New Hampshire, South Carolina, Florida and California. If she runs the tables there, the nomination almost certainly will be hers.

Yet in Iowa, the state that will kick off the voting in precinct caucuses one night in January, she's still in a three-person race with John Edwards and Barack Obama.

And history suggests that anything can happen there in the final weeks as more voters tune in. Iowa voters tend to see the top candidates as similar on the hot-button issues. Voters are signaling in interviews that they're more interested in whether a candidate can win the general election and how he or she would govern.

Most Iowa Democrats interviewed at random in recent days like or admire Clinton. Many think her experience in Washington as a first lady and senator would give her an edge in pushing the Democratic agenda through Congress and into law. But some Iowa Democrats harbor doubts about whether Clinton's political baggage would cost them the

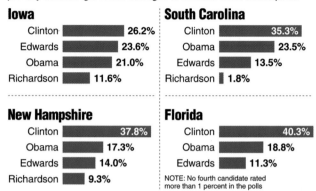

Leading Democratic candidates '08

How the top Democratic presidential candidates are doing in early primary states. Figures are averages of a state's most recent polls.

Iowa
Clinton	26.2%
Edwards	23.6%
Obama	21.0%
Richardson	11.6%

South Carolina
Clinton	35.3%
Obama	23.5%
Edwards	13.5%
Richardson	1.8%

New Hampshire
Clinton	37.8%
Obama	17.3%
Edwards	14.0%
Richardson	9.3%

Florida
Clinton	40.3%
Obama	18.8%
Edwards	11.3%

NOTE: No fourth candidate rated more than 1 percent in the polls

Source: Real Clear Politics poll averages; Iowa: average of five polls, Aug. 17-Sept. 10, 2007, 462-600 likely Democratic voters; N.H.: average of four polls, Aug. 26-Sept. 16, 2007, 403-618 likely Democratic voters; S.C.: average of four polls, Aug. 20-Sept. 10, 2007, 313-600 likely Democratic voters; Fla.: average of four polls, Aug. 10-Sept. 10, 2007, 446-1,200 likely Democratic voters
Graphic: Angela Smith, Judy Treible © 2007 MCT

general election.

Many are also drawn to Obama and his lofty appeal to more civil politics.

But a lot of people think he's too inexperienced to be president.

"It's not his time," said Cindy Forbes of Urbandale, a suburb of Des Moines. "He's not experienced enough. He'll be president someday, but not now."

-- By Steven Thomma/
McClatchy Washington Bureau

Clinton, Obama sell economic visions on campaign trail

Portsmouth, New Hampshire: October 8, 2007

Barack Obama today rolled out an ambitious energy plan aimed at curbing greenhouse gases and reducing dependence on foreign oil.

Obama joined Hillary Clinton and John Edwards in favoring a cap-and-trade program to curb global warming. They would set a cap on total carbon emissions, then set corporate pollution allowances within that cap. Companies could buy other firms' unused quotas to pollute more. All three Democrats call for reducing carbon emissions to 80 percent below 1990 levels by 2050. But Obama's plan goes further than his rivals': He would make oil, coal and

gas companies pay for all of their emissions quotas.

"Businesses don't own the sky, the public does," he said.

Obama set a goal of reducing U.S. oil consumption by at least 35 percent by 2030. He compared his plan to President Franklin Roosevelt's wartime production oversight and John Kennedy's moon program.

"I will set big goals for this country as president, some so large that the technology to reach them does not yet exist," Obama said. "But that has not stopped us before."

-- Margaret Talev/
McClatchy Washington Bureau

Obama and Clinton awaited questions at Univision's Democratic Presidential Forum at the University of Miami in Coral Gables, Florida, in September 2007. (Patrick Farrell/Miami Herald/MCT)

A master at engaging the crowd

Washington, D.C.: November 18, 2007

In February 1981, at the small, mostly white college he was attending in Los Angeles, 19-year-old Barack Obama tried something that shaped the course of his life.

He gave a speech.

Like many students of that era, the sophomore was drawn to the South African divestment movement, which demanded that college trustees drop institutional investments that supported the racial segregation system known as apartheid. Obama's role at the Occidental College rally that warm winter day was to grab the crowd's attention, then be whisked off by students in paramilitary costumes.

"He was so composed in his arguments that I think after that speech a lot of people wondered, 'Who is that guy and why haven't we heard more from him?'" recalled Rebecca Rivera, a classmate.

That debut speech was a turning point; it set a template for revealing a rare talent.

Nearly a quarter-century later, another Obama speech, this one at the 2004 Democratic National Convention, transformed him into an American political phenomenon. It launched him from being an obscure state lawmaker into a celebrity U.S. senator from Illinois and gave him a springboard to become a challenger for his party's 2008 presidential nomination.

While Democratic and Republican rivals campaign on their military heroism, governing resumes, private-sector success or White House ties, what sets Obama apart most is how he engages audiences, physically and emotionally.

He seems to hug and shake a crowd at once. On the campaign trail, he has a crisp, resonant voice combined with an easy, self-effacing manner. Tall, slim, with exceptionally long fingers, he juxtaposes a physical sense of calm with disarmingly emotional strings of words. His presence lets him lift a vague stump speech about hope into something that seems much weightier, at least in the moment.

Hearing his own voice that day at Occidental seemed to spark Obama's political awakening.

"I knew I had them (aspirations), that the connection had been made," Obama wrote of that day in his memoir *Dreams from My Father*. "I really wanted to stay up there, to hear my voice bouncing off the crowd and returning back to me in applause. I had so much left to say."

Yet it also exposed a struggle in him between ego and guilt, and afterward came a rush of shame.

"The whole thing was a farce . . . and me and my one-minute oration — the biggest farce of all." But a friend's rebuke of his cynicism triggered guilt, which led him to more advocacy.

Obama soon followed a path to politics. He transferred within months to Columbia University. He spent a few years as a community organizer in Chicago. He joined a church. He went to Harvard Law School, where he became the first black president of the Law Review. Next came a do-good job at a civil rights law firm and work as a constitutional law professor.

His presence lets him lift a vague stump speech about hope into something that seems much weightier, at least in the moment.

Election to the Illinois Senate followed, then a failed bid for the U.S. House of Representatives and a shoot-the-moon campaign for an open U.S. Senate seat. He won, helped greatly by his opponents' flameouts. Finally came the invitation to give "the speech" in 2004, after Democratic presidential nominee John Kerry determined that Obama projected the right image.

Judson Miner, who heads the liberal Chicago civil rights firm that hired Obama after Harvard, said the first time he had lunch with his recruit, he was so struck by Obama's thought process and by how he drew others into conversation that, "I told my wife I just had lunch with one of the most extraordinary people I'd met."

"This was a guy who was interested in having an impact with things," Miner said. "I think he was really wrestling with, how can you be most effective? As a lawyer? In some other role? We never talked about politics, but I wasn't surprised when he came to me a few years later and said there was this opportunity in the state Senate."

Miner enthusiastically supports Obama's presidential bid.

"If he had a fault, which I guess sometimes manifests itself on the campaign trail, he instinctively

Obama talked to voters at a campaign stop in Coralville, Iowa. (Chuck Kennedy/MCT)

Obama speaking supporters in Boone, Iowa. (Chuck Kennedy/MCT)

appreciates all the nuances of things," Miner said. "He's decisive, but that processing involves wrestling with these things a little bit. And sometimes that's not a good trait for a politician."

Obama's critics see bigger flaws in his judgment, which they chalk up to a combination of inexperience and sanctimony.

One involves a 2005 land deal first reported by *The Chicago Tribune*. Obama and the wife of Tony Rezko, a politically connected Chicago developer who has since been indicted in connection with paying kickbacks, bought adjacent plots of land on the same day. Months later, Obama bought back part of the Rezko parcel to expand his $1.65 million home's lot.

The revelation stunned government watchdogs because in the Illinois Senate and on Capitol Hill Obama flaunted his reputation as a clean-government champion. He has urged tighter fundraising and disclosure rules and railed against getting too cozy with lobbyists.

Obama, who had known Rezko since the early 1990s, later said it was "boneheaded" of him not to anticipate how the sale would look; he returned Rezko's contributions. Critics have found no evidence that he did legislative favors for Rezko.

But Cindi Canary, the executive director of the Illinois Campaign for Political Reform, said the deal still gave her pause.

"More than anything else, there was a sense that Senator Obama should have known better," she said.

"One is judged by the company one keeps. Tony Rezko was a very well-known wheeler and dealer in Illinois politics, someone who for a number of years had a swirl of trouble around him and allegations before the final indictment came down."

Rival Democrats have painted him as too green on foreign policy to serve as a wartime president.

Obama raises the experience question in his own campaign speeches, painting his rivals as cynics and arguing that his mix of youth, background diversity and civic engagement would better serve the nation.

Voters often ask Obama which president he admires most. He usually says Abraham Lincoln, who ended slavery, managed the country through civil war — and delivered one of history's most famous speeches, the Gettysburg Address.

But Obama sometimes betrays a yearning to be viewed like John Kennedy, to set a style of leadership that reinvigorates public faith in government.

"One of my jobs as president is to make government cool again," Obama told an engaged college crowd in New Hampshire this fall.

Because of Kennedy, Obama said, "thousands of young people were inspired to say, 'I want to give something back; I want to serve.' Now we're losing that. And we've got to restore it."

— Margaret Talev/
McClatchy Washington Bureau

An interview with Michelle Obama

In Columbia, South Carolina, Michelle Obama spoke to a crowd at Dreher High School in November 2007. (Gerry Melendez/The State, Columbia, South Carolina)

Orangeburg, South Carolina: November 21, 2007

Between campaign appearances for her husband this week in South Carolina, Michelle Obama, 43, a woman, a lawyer, a hospital executive and the mother of girls Malia and Sasha, 9 and 6, sat down for a few questions with McClatchy's Margaret Talev.

QUESTION: Explain the choice and the issues that black voters are confronting (in whether to support Barack Obama's candidacy) that white voters aren't confronting.

ANSWER: People who are oppressed at every turn in their world, they see indications directly or indirectly of what they can't do. You see negative images about yourself on TV. This is what you take in as a person of color. It feeds on that self-doubt — it builds on it and it makes you think that somehow, something must be wrong with me and others like me so that we're not ready, and we're not good enough to be anywhere, let alone running for president of the United States. Folks don't want to be disappointed; they don't want Barack to be emotionally disappointed by what they

perceive to be other people who won't accept the possibilities of who he is. Sometimes it's easier not to try at all than to try and fail.

Q: Was this a revelation to you?
A: No, it's my life. It doesn't go away because you reach a certain age or a certain professional standing. That is a part of who you are. I struggle less because I have had exposure to the powers that be; I've sat at the table, as has Barack, with the best of the best. And then you look around and go, "What was the big deal?"

Q: Do you think merely having an African-American president would diminish racism in the country?
A: When I go to Iowa and I stand in front of a small community and I tell them my story and I talk about my dad (who had multiple sclerosis and is deceased) and our values, you know, there is no difference. And the fact that they see me, this tall black woman and they say, "I know her, she is very familiar to me." (It) breaks down barriers and misperceptions that exist

because people just don't know each other.

Q: What are some issues, whether they're domestic issues or international, issues that are very important to you or that you just feel are under-discussed?

A: Things haven't evolved completely for men and women in relationships. Women are stuck in this sort of, "OK, I am now working, but there are societal pressures that I still maintain this role." We all have those folks in our lives who are saying, "But this is what a woman does and you're doing something else." So now we're trying to do it all and we're driving ourselves crazy, because something's got to give. That's something that I talk a lot about and what I'd like to talk about in my role as first lady. It's this work-family balance, because this is something I see that cuts across all socioeconomic classes, all races, all political (persuasions). Women in this world are drowning in our situations. I still think women are pretending like, "I can do it all." First, it's to say, "No, you can't, and you're not crazy if you can't." But the other thing, these are domestic agendas. We need decent health care, better schools. We need jobs that pay a living wage.

Q: Who did your husband look to as a role model in becoming a dad since his dad really wasn't around?

A: He had his grandfather, who he grew up with, and his mother's second husband, Lolo. When he was alive and they were together, he was very much a father figure. Like many young kids who don't have fathers in their lives, you look to the men around you.

Q: Do you think that marriages have changed and the role of a spouse is more one of friendship and irreverence?

A: I think obviously marriages have evolved. When I look at my grandparents and how they interacted . . . My grandmother who passed, I'd be in the middle of some case or working on some project, and I'd call Grandma and it'd be Sunday and it'd be my only day off and she'd say, "So, whatcha cooking?" And I'm like, "Mmm, nothing, Grandma. I'm not cooking."

Q: Does your husband cook? I've heard he at least has a chili recipe.

A: I cook, but . . . he can cook. The chili recipe, it's his. I stole it from him. It's lots of good spices and lots of meats and beans. You put lots of cheese on it.

Michelle Obama in Columbia, South Carolina. (Gerry Melendez/The State/Columbia, South Carolina)

He also has this sort of mixed Thai dish — I don't know that recipe. It's got vegetables and chicken and cashews. It's really pretty good.

Q: I read Lauryn Hill is on your iPod?

A: I do love Lauryn Hill. I love Jill Scott. I'm lovin' Beyonce. My girls are loving Beyonce. Believe it or not, we listen to her CD every day going to school. Stevie Wonder is my most favorite anything of everybody. If I'm on a deserted island, I want "Songs in the Key of Life," I want "Innervisions." I want Stevie's albums.

Q: What about (your husband)?

A: Stevie's huge. But he's listening to a little Jay-Z, and he loves jazz — Coltrane, Miles Davis.

As Obama rises in polls, Clinton lashes out

Cedar Rapids, Iowa: December 2, 2007

Hillary Clinton questioned the courage and character of her chief opponent today in the wake of a poll finding her campaign was losing ground in this crucial early-voting state.

A new *Des Moines Register* poll showed Clinton trailing Obama, 28 percent to 25 percent. In October, the poll showed Clinton leading Obama, 29 percent to 22 percent. In both polls, John Edwards was at 23 percent.

With the Iowa caucuses one month away, Clinton unleashed her harshest critique yet of Obama, saying he "blinked" in offering a health care plan that didn't give all Americans coverage and is being disingenuous as he touts it. And Clinton questioned whether Obama's political action committee was violating Federal Election Commission rules.

Obama dismissed Clinton's broadside, saying it was prompted by his rise in the polls.

Clinton says her plan would cover all Americans and criticized Obama for offering a plan that, many independent analysts say, could leave as many as 15 million Americans uninsured. Currently, about 45 million Americans lack health insurance.

Clinton mocked Obama for describing his plan in different ways: "It's universal, or virtually universal, or comprehensive. It's obvious that he doesn't want to face up to the very position he took, because every time he changes his posture. At some point you've got to ask yourself, who's really committed here?"

As for the political action committee, Clinton said that, based on legal advice, she shut down her own leadership PAC when she decided to run for president. In 2006, her PAC, HillPAC, distributed tens of thousands of dollars to Democratic candidates across the country. It has been reported that Obama's PAC, Hopefund, this year distributed tens of thousands of dollars to candidates in key states like Iowa and New Hampshire. Such PACs, known as leadership PACs, are routinely used by politicians to curry favor with other politicians.

Obama called Clinton's attacks on his PAC "outlandish accusations."

"Everything that we've done is in exact accordance with the law," Obama said at a press conference in Des Moines.

Clinton indicated to reporters that she hoped more attacks on Obama would fuel her comeback.

"Now the fun part starts," she declared. "We're into the last month, and we're going to start drawing a contrast, because I want every Iowan to have accurate information when they make their decisions."

Later, Obama issued a statement decrying Clinton for saying the coming weeks would be "fun."

"Washington insiders might think throwing mud is fun, but the American people are looking for leadership that can unite this country," Obama said.

-- Matt Stearns/McClatchy Washington Bureau

Again, Clinton turns up the heat

Clear Lake, Iowa: December 3, 2007

Saying the country needed "a doer, not a talker" in the White House, Hillary Clinton today mocked Barack Obama's record in public office. In points that she had once left to surrogates to make, Clinton disparaged Obama for "present" votes while serving in the Illinois legislature.

"It's kind of like voting 'maybe,'" Clinton said. "A president can't pick and choose which challenges he or she will face...."

Obama voted "present" in 1997 on two bills that would have outlawed the procedure that some call partial-birth abortion and on two 2001 bills related to parental notification of minors seeking abortions. He voted "present" on a 1999 bill that would have made firing a gun on or near school grounds a crime and on a 2001 bill that would have kept strip clubs from opening within 1,000 yards of schools, churches and daycare centers.

Clinton wondered aloud whether it made sense to "put America in the hands of someone with little national or international experience who started running for president as soon as he arrived in the United States Senate."

The Obama campaign didn't rebut statistics regarding his voting record in Illinois, but noted that his "present" votes on abortion issues were cast with the support of the president of the Illinois Planned Parenthood Council.

--Matt Stearns/McClatchy Washington Bureau

With Oprah Winfrey and Michelle Obama looking on, Barack Obama addressed a crowd of 29,000 at a stadium in Columbia, South Carolina. (C. Aluka Berry/The State)

Tapping the power of Oprah

Columbia, South Carolina: December 10, 2007

In what Barack Obama described as the best-attended rally of the political season for any candidate, more than 29,000 attendees jammed Williams-Brice Stadium today.

Media mogul Oprah Winfrey rallied the crowd of supporters — a primarily female and African-American audience — to get behind her friend Obama. She called him a new kind of leader who possessed "a tongue dipped in the unvarnished truth."

Winfrey, who had never endorsed a presidential candidate, said she was "stepping out of my pew" because she had been disappointed with politicians but had become inspired by Obama's message of change and unity.

"Dr. King dreamed the dream, but we don't have to dream the dream anymore," Oprah told the crowd. "We get to vote that dream into office."

Conjecture has been heavy as to whether the endorsement of a popular and influential personality like Winfrey — whose book club endorsements have created best-sellers — would help Obama. The talk show host put the issue front and center during her introductory remarks, telling the crowd:

"I'm not here to tell you what to think. I got some sense. I know the difference between a book club and this seminal moment in our history."

Polling shows that one-third to one-half of likely Democratic voters in the Palmetto State have yet to choose a candidate.

Despite Obama's increasingly critical rhetoric about Hillary Clinton at other campaign events, he fired no shots her way today. But Winfrey did, saying that a candidate's spending time in Washington wasn't an important factor "unless they're accountable for the judgments they made with that time."

Both Winfrey and Obama personalized their message to the South Carolina audience. Winfrey mentioned her Southern roots in Mississippi and Tennessee and growing up as a regular churchgoer. Obama followed suit. In addition to the Chicagoan's liberal use of the word "y'all," he spoke of his wife visiting family members in Georgetown while she was growing up and his own trips around the state.

Ultimately, the campaign was looking to spread Obama's message beyond the stadium. Each attendee received a sheet listing four registered South Carolina voters and a phone script. Attendees were asked to call the voters on their sheet — right then and there — and ask them to support Obama in the primary.

— Gina Smith/
The State, Columbia, South Carolina

The sparring goes off-camera

Johnston, Iowa
December 13, 2007

Barack Obama and Hillary Clinton dealt offstage today with the fallout from their close contest while onstage all the Democratic presidential candidates made nice for television in a polite debate.

The 90-minute debate was the last chance for the six major candidates to face one another before voting starts in Iowa on January 3. With three candidates neck and neck and neck for first place in the state — Hillary Clinton, Barack Obama and John Edwards — none dared personally attack a rival for fear of a backlash from Iowa voters. Thus the event did little to alter the shape of the campaign.

Off-camera, however, Clinton's campaign looked for ways to slow Obama's momentum, which has washed away her narrow lead in Iowa and her larger lead in New Hampshire.

Yesterday, Clinton's national campaign co-chairman called attention to Obama's admitted use of illegal drugs as a teen. Today, Clinton apologized to her Senate colleague.

The apology came this morning as both prepared to board their private jets at Washington's Reagan National Airport to fly to Iowa for the debate. Obama strategist David Axelrod said that Clinton sent an aide over first to say she wanted to speak to Obama, then she walked over herself.

Clinton, who earlier called this the "fun part" of the campaign, told Obama she didn't authorize or approve of the comments from her co-chairman, Bill Shaheen.

Axelrod said that Obama accepted the apology, but that the senator also delivered a strong message to Clinton.

"What Senator Obama expressed to Senator Clinton is that it's important we send a message to our campaign up and down the line: It's not fun, this is not sport, to try and attack opponents in these kinds of ways," Axelrod said. "You've got to send that signal from the top."

Later in the day, Shaheen resigned as Clinton's campaign co-chairman. The campaign issued a statement in his name, which said in part: "I would like to reiterate that I deeply regret my comments yesterday and say again that they were in no way authorized by Senator Clinton or the Clinton campaign."

The debate offered only one exchange between Clinton and Obama.

When the moderator asked Obama how he, a

Clinton talked to supporters in Mason City, Iowa, in December 2007. (Chuck Kennedy/MCT)

novice at foreign policy, would foster change when he's relying on advice from several of former President Bill Clinton's foreign-policy advisers, Hillary Clinton spoke up from across the stage.

"I want to hear that," she said, then erupted into loud laughter.

"Well, Hillary," Obama responded, "I'm looking forward to you advising me as well."

Throughout the rest of the debate, the candidates all tended to agree with one another.

— Steven Thomma/
McClatchy Washington Bureau

A legion of youth is enlisted

Des Moines, Iowa: December 14, 2007

Amina Kader is only 17, but as the leader of the Barack Obama student group at Hoover High School, she's a foot soldier in the Democratic presidential candidate's infantry in the first state to vote.

All the major candidates in both parties are courting young voters to varying degrees, especially on college campuses. But Obama — who polls indicate has the most to gain if students show up to caucus in Iowa — appears to be building an unmatched network throughout Iowa's high schools.

His campaign Web site lists 144 Iowa high schools with Obama student groups. That's 40 percent of the state's public high schools, and it translates to thousands of teens who say they're committed to

Obama meeting with supporters in Jefferson, Iowa. (Chuck Kennedy/ MCT)

caucusing for Obama. The group at Hoover High has about 25 active members. On the Web site, students can check out a map and a pull-down bar with contact information about their school's Obama groups or how to start one.

Iowans as young as 17 can caucus provided they'll turn 18 by next year's general election. It's a significant pool: An estimated 38,500 high schoolers are eligible to caucus in the state's 1,784 precincts. That's comparable to the combined student populations of Iowa State University and the University of Northern Iowa.

Overall, Iowa has roughly 2 million registered voters, but fewer than one in five typically turn out to caucus.

Obama's high school effort is driven partly by resources — he has enough young adult volunteers in Iowa to assign them to work with schools — and partly by the campaign's uncertainty about how the timing of this year's caucuses could affect the already unreliable college vote. The January 3 caucuses fall smack in the middle of campus holiday breaks.

One theory has it that this could help less traditional candidates such as Obama by scattering college voters home to smaller precincts where their votes could count more than they would in more populous areas. The counter-theory says that most out-of-state students won't return to Iowa early just to caucus, and that many in-state students will be away on vacation.

In 2004, 18-to-24-year-olds constituted only 3.9 percent of Democratic caucus-goers in Iowa.

This year, college Democratic and Republican clubs are scurrying to boost turnout by organizing carpools for out-of-state students who want to come back to caucus, handing out pamphlets explaining that in-state students can caucus in hometown precincts and lobbying their campuses to reopen for a day or two.

Still, Chelsea Hottovy, 21, a student at Drake University in Des Moines whose family lives in Nebraska, says she has strong feelings about the election but no plans to caucus: "I don't really understand what gets accomplished, so I don't really feel like it's that good a use of my time."

"Students just aren't that attached to the electoral process," said Dennis Goldford, a political science professor at Drake. "It would shock me if there were a major increase."

But high school students?

Their winter breaks are much shorter and they live with their parents, so they're more likely to be home to caucus.

Some Iowa high school civics teachers are requiring that seniors caucus or volunteer a certain number of hours with a campaign of their choice.

— *Margaret Talev/*
McClatchy Washington Bureau

The way of the '08 campaign: technology

Columbia, South Carolina: December 22, 2007

Everyone had laptops and handheld devices at the ready when Obama visied Google's headquarters in Mountain View, California, in late 2007. Across the country, candidates were casting a wide tech net. (Brian Baer/Sacramento Bee/MCT)

Elizabeth Bentley of Greenville, South Carolina, was attempting to persuade a co-worker to vote for Barack Obama.

"She wanted to know about Obama's stance on tax reform, and I didn't know all of the details," Bentley said. So Bentley whipped out her cell phone, sent a text message to Obama's campaign and, in less than a minute, had an answer.

"My co-worker was really impressed," Bentley said.

Welcome to the new technology-drenched political world where setting up a Web site or blasting a generic e-mail into cyberspace is so last century. Instead, the presidential candidates of this election season are using their technology tools like a surgeon's blade, carving out personalized responses designed for segments of the voting community.

With its roots in Republican John McCain's 2000 presidential campaign and Democrat Howard Dean's 2004 Internet-embraced run, technology has made video posts, news clips and blogs staples of a candidate's Web site. It has also made the good, old cell phone a campaign tool — a godsend in a poor state like South Carolina.

"There are people who may not have a computer, may not have a home phone, but just about everyone has a cell phone," said Jeremy Bird, Obama's field director for South Carolina. "(Texting) is another way to communicate with people where they are and how they prefer to receive information."

For the voter who wants constant updates, the campaigns have them covered. One of this season's interactive darlings is Twitter, a social media tool that allows candidates to be hyper-connected to voters and constantly answer their questions — "What are you doing now? How about now? And now?"

— *Gina Smith/The State, Columbia, South Carolina*

Long preliminaries over, voters' time has come

Des Moines, Iowa: January 2, 2008

Now, at last, it's the voters' turn.

Starting tomorrow in Iowa and followed by a blur of state-by-state voting over the next months, the American people begin picking presidential candidates for the two major political parties and charting a new course for the country.

They do so after the longest, costliest election run-up in American history, the first since 1920 with no heir apparent in either party. Both parties are eager to turn the page on the George W. Bush era, particularly Democrats angry about the Iraq war, but also Republicans unhappy about such issues as illegal immigration.

As the voting neared, candidates made their final pitches today to Iowans in ubiquitous television ads and dashed around the snow-covered state by bus and plane, trying to inspire their supporters to turn out for the caucuses. By now, the campaign story line is familiar to Iowans, who have been inundated since last January. Campaigns and interest groups spent more than $20 million on TV ads that appeared more than 10,000 times. Candidates visited Iowa towns more than 2,000 times.

Barack Obama raced to five rallies across eastern and central Iowa before closing the day before midnight at a Des Moines high school where a group of students support him. He appealed to newcomers to the political process — young people, independents, people who had never gone to a precinct caucus — to propel him to victory. And he dared them to prove the pundits wrong.

"They don't think you're going to show up!" he told a rally near the University of Iowa. "Are you going to prove 'em wrong?" he asked to cheers.

John Edwards finished his long courtship of Iowa Democrats with a marathon, 36-hour bus trip and a caucus-eve concert with singer John Mellencamp.

Hillary Clinton barnstormed the state by jet, pitching her experience at stop after stop and on TV.

"After all the town meetings, the pie and coffee, it comes down to this: Who is ready to be president and ready to start solving the big challenges we face on day one?" Clinton said in a two-minute ad.

— *Steven Thomma/McClatchy Washington Bureau*

Obama greeted backers on a caucus-eve stop in Coralville, Iowa. (Chuck Kennedy/MCT)

Well into their long slugging match for the Democratic nomination, Hillary Clinton waited for Obama to finish making his point at a debate in Austin, Texas, on February 21, 2008. (Tom Pennington/Fort Worth Star-Telegram/MCT)

THE BATTLE IS JOINED

In huge numbers, Iowans speak
Obama No. 1, Edwards No. 2, Clinton No. 3

Des Moines, Iowa: January 3, 2008

Barack Obama of Illinois won the first test of the 2008 presidential campaign tonight as Democrats surged to Iowa's precinct caucuses in record numbers.

His victory over Hillary Clinton and John Edwards, two far more familiar and practiced politicians, suggested a hunger among Democrats for a new voice and perhaps a new approach to politics.

In a victory speech, Obama said: "They said this day would never come. They said our sights were just

As CNN declared Obama would win Iowa, Wanda Van Wyk of Prairie City, Iowa, cheered at Obama's victory party in Des Moines. Facing page: Obama and his daughter Malia waved to the crowd. (Brian Baer/Sacramento Bee/MCT)

too high. They said this country was too divided, too disillusioned to ever come together around a common purpose. But on this January night, at this defining moment in history, you have done what the cynics said we couldn't do."

Obama had 38 percent of the delegates, Edwards 30 percent, Clinton 29 percent, Bill Richardson 2 percent and Joe Biden 1 percent. Biden and Chris Dodd abandoned their campaigns.

Though Iowa was only the first event of what could be a long campaign, Obama's victory signaled that Democrats were willing to embrace the first leader of a new generation.

Clinton, as the yearlong national frontrunner and the most admired Democrat in the country, according to national polls, suffered a major setback by failing to win. Nevertheless, she has the money and support to fight on, and she left no doubt that she intended to do so.

"We're going to take this enthusiasm and go right to New Hampshire," Clinton told cheering supporters at a Des Moines hotel. "I am as ready as I can be."

Obama and Clinton probably now will have to duel state by state. Edwards doesn't have the money and the nationwide organization of his two prime rivals, and he could find that anything less than victory in New Hampshire will dry up his resources. Still, he too vowed to keep going.

Democratic Party officials said the attendance at the town hall-like meetings soared to 227,000, a dramatic increase from the record 124,000 who attended four years ago and sent John Kerry on his way to the Democratic nomination.

Their hunger for change fueled Obama's victory. Polls of Democrats entering the caucuses showed 51 percent were looking for someone who could change politics. Of them, 51 percent went for Obama. Far fewer cited experience, a blow to Clinton, who has built her campaign on that claim.

Obama ran as the fresh voice of American politics — with the strikingly different African-American face to match. He promised a new tone and a more civil approach to getting things done in Washington. And he played a generational card, saying it was time to retire a baby-boom generation that came of age in the 1960s and retained its combative politics.

His message struck a chord with young Iowans, who turned out in droves for his rallies. They also helped send Obama to victory, apparently defying the history that said young people don't show up to caucus here. Polls showed Obama winning 57 percent of the support from those age 29 and younger.

On the Republican side, Mike Huckabee won 35 percent of the delegates to Mitt Romney's 25 percent. Fred Thompson and John McCain tied at 13 percent.

— Steven Thomma/ McClatchy Washington Bureau

When hope and history meshed

Des Moines, Iowa: January 4, 2008

He spent the morning of the Iowa caucuses doing what he has loved since he was a kid named Barry growing up in Hawaii: playing basketball with friends. But by day's end, as Barack Obama ascended the stage to give his victory speech,

Supporters clapped their hands over their heads in Des Moines after Obama's victory in Iowa. (Brian Baer/Sacramento Bee/MCT)

he couldn't pretend that anything was ordinary anymore.

At 46, the freshman U.S. senator from Chicago had undeniably made history as the first African-American to win the caucuses in this rural and almost entirely white state. He arguably become the front-runner for his party's presidential nomination.

"Years from now," he told his supporters, his voice hoarse, "you'll be able to look back with pride and say this was the moment when it all began.... This was the moment when we tore down barriers that have divided us for too long."

It was a stunning achievement for a senator with virtually no foreign policy experience running in a time of war and globalization, and for a candidate who was unknown nationally until he captured the nation's attention with a speech at the 2004 Democratic National Convention.

His themes of hope and change, his promise to govern in a bipartisan spirit and to unite races and cultures, his argument that he had opposed the Iraq war from the outset, unlike Hillary Clinton and John Edwards, all helped boost Obama, especially with young voters and independents. His supporters were ecstatic as they filed into the hall to wait for him, most already having heard of his victory as they drove in.

"Change has arrived, that's right!" said Shannon Coleman, a 38-year-old African-American school employee who arrived with her husband, John, a 35-year-old white truck driver. "To me, it's from the Bible: It took 40 years in the desert ...."

Her husband finished her thought: "The Israelites, a trip that should have taken two weeks or three weeks, took 40 years," John Coleman said. "It represents history. Who built America? It was a mix of races of people."

Said Stephanie Asklof, 56, a white caucus-goer, "We've come to a point where people are really not looking at race — they're looking at character, ideas, the ability to be the uniter."

The rowdy crowd kept erupting in claps and cheers as TV screens projected Obama the winner.

"Fired up. Ready to go," they chanted. "O-BA-MA, O-BA-MA."

Obama was having dinner at a steak restaurant in West Des Moines when he learned that the TV networks had projected he was the winner.

As he took the stage with his wife and their two daughters, his face was beaming but his body language was calm and cool. He waved and clapped. The speakers blared global activist band U-2, then Stevie Wonder.

And as the crowd dispersed, it was Brooks & Dunn's "Only in America."

— Margaret Talev/
McClatchy Washington Bureau

Three days before the New Hampshire primary, hundreds of people lined up in the snow outside Nashua North High School for an Obama rally. (Chuck Kennedy/MCT)

The debate grows lively

Goffstown, New Hampshire: January 5, 2008

Hillary Clinton tore into Barack Obama in a spirited debate tonight, accusing her rival of changing positions often, notably on health care.

"As the AP described it, he could have a pretty good debate with himself," Clinton said.

Obama hit right back, suggesting that the Associated Press had been "quoting some of your folks, Hillary," and chiding everyone not to "distort each other's records as Election Day approaches here in New Hampshire."

John Edwards jumped in too: "I didn't hear these kinds of attacks from Senator Clinton when she was ahead."

"I've been in hostage negotiations that were a lot more civil than this," quipped New Mexico Gov. Bill Richardson.

The clash among the four Democrats was their first since Obama trounced Clinton in the Iowa caucuses two days ago, and the last before New Hampshire voters cast the nation's first secret ballots for presidential nominees three days from now.

Obama is leading narrowly in many New Hampshire polls; Clinton had counted on winning the two early states to create an aura of inevitability. Instead, she's fighting for her political life.

Not all the exchanges were hostile. At one point, Clinton was asked why people seemed to like Obama more than her.

"Well, that hurts my feelings," she said, smiling in a self-deprecating way. The audience laughed. "But I'll try to go on. He's very likeable. I agree with that. I don't think I'm that bad."

"You're likeable enough," Obama said quietly.

Later, however, after Edwards and Obama bragged about how much they had challenged special interests and achieved change over the years, Clinton interrupted:

"Can we have a reality break for a minute?" she said. She challenged Obama again for voting for an energy bill containing tax breaks for special interests.

"Words are not action," she said. "And as beautifully presented and passionately felt as they are, they are not action. We have to translate talk into action."

— *David Lightman/*
McClatchy Washington Bureau

Briefer speeches and bolder criticism

Manchester, New Hampshire: January 6, 2008

Fighting for a political comeback, Hillary Clinton retooled her campaign for New Hampshire primary voters today with a sharp attack on rival Barack Obama. Clinton found herself on the ropes just two days before New Hampshire's primary. A new McClatchy-MSNBC poll showed the New York senator was in danger of a second straight loss to the Illinois senator.

Speaking to overflow rallies and going door to door, Clinton hammered Obama as offering a mixed record in the Senate and nothing but talk about what he'd do in the White House.

Hillary Clinton campaigning in Durham, New Hampshire. (Chuck Kennedy/MCT)

"There's a big difference between talking and action, between talking and performing, and I am going to make that case to as many people in New Hampshire as I possibly can," she said here.

She ripped him for voting for the Patriot Act, "for Dick Cheney's energy bill," for continued funding of the Iraq war, and for criticizing lobbyists while letting a lobbyist chair his New Hampshire campaign.

"That's not change," she said. Going door to door, Clinton said she felt good about the new tactics and the prospects for the primary.

Clinton's campaign also said it had made negative TV ads and bought the time to air them, and was debating whether to broadcast them. A mailing attacking Obama for his "present" vote on an abortion bill in the Illinois state Senate started arriving in mailboxes over the weekend.

She also overhauled her approach to voters, cutting her stump speech from 55 minutes to 15, and opening herself to more than an hour of questions instead. Aides thought the shift played to her strength discussing policy rather than a losing fight with Obama for rhetorical style.

Obama brushed aside the new criticisms.

"One of my opponents said we can't just, you know, offer the American people false hopes about what we can get done," he said at a Manchester theater. "The real gamble in this election is to do the same things, with the same folks, playing the same games over and over and over again and somehow expect a different result.... It is time to turn the page."

John Edwards spent the day trying to convince voters that he's still in the race, that it's really between Obama and him.

On the Republican side, the McClatchy-MSNBC poll showed the contest close in both parties. Mitt Romney fought to regain the lead he'd enjoyed for months in the state, casting himself as a can-do outsider most able to change Washington and slamming John McCain as an insider often disloyal to the party.

Confident of victory, McCain declared flatly, "I will win," and worked to avoid battling back and forth with Romney. He did get in one swipe:

"He has changed his position on almost every major issue. That doesn't mean he's not a good person."

— Steven Thomma and other members of the McClatchy Washington Bureau

At a cafe in Portsmouth, Hillary Clinton listened to a group of undecided voters. (Chuck Kennedy/MCT)

A tear wells up

Portsmouth, New Hampshire: January 7, 2008

Hillary Clinton battled hard, and at times emotionally, today to try to prevent a Barack Obama victory in tomorrow's New Hampshire primary. A notable moment came when she talked to a small group of undecided voters at Cafe Espresso.

Marianne Pernold Young, a photographer, asked her, "How do you do it? How do you ... keep upbeat and so wonderful?"

As Clinton began to answer, her voice began to break and tears appeared in her eyes.

"You know, this is very personal for me," she said. "It's not just political and it's not just public. I see what's happening, and we have to reverse it."

Clinton has fallen behind Obama in the polls. He has an average lead of 8 percentage points in 11 different statewide polls that surveyed through the weekend. Clinton's pitch was that she's the candidate with toughness and experience. At a community center in Dover, she said: "There's a big difference between talk and action. There's a big difference

between rhetoric and reality."

Obama spoke at the Lebanon Opera house, where his high-energy closing argument centered on his two central campaign themes, change and hope.

Without naming Clinton, he zeroed in on her suggestion at a debate that he couldn't deliver on his promises.

"One of my opponents said, ugh, stop giving people false hopes about what we can accomplish. False hopes? False hopes? There's no such thing. This country was built on hope. Was JFK looking up at the moon and saying, 'Ah, false hope, too far.'?

"Reality check? Dr. (Martin Luther) King, standing on the steps of the Lincoln Memorial, looking out over that magnificent crowd, the Reflecting Pool, the Washington Monument: 'Sorry guys, false hope. The dream will die.' False hope? We don't need leaders to tell us what we can't do; we need those who can inspire us to do."

— *David Lightman and William Douglas/*
McClatchy Washington Bureau

A jolt from New Hampshire
It's Clinton — and coast-to-coast struggle ahead

Manchester, New Hampshire: January 8, 2008

Hillary Clinton surged back from a distant second in weekend polls to stun rising star Barack Obama and win New Hampshire's Democratic presidential primary today.

The New York senator had 39 percent to Obama's

After winning the New Hampshire primary, Hillary Clinton thanked her supporters. (Christopher Kezer/MCT)

36 percent. John Edwards was a distant third with 17 percent.

Pre-primary polls had suggested that Clinton would lose big, perhaps by double digits. But she ran strong among women and voters over 40, while the Illinois senator failed to get the overwhelming backing from younger voters who helped propel him to victory last week in Iowa.

The Clinton comeback — reminiscent of her husband's rebound in the 1992 New Hampshire primary, when he climbed to a second-place finish and went on to win the White House — sets up a coast-to-coast duel for the Democratic nomination.

Beaming as she looked over a sea of cheering supporters, she embraced her husband, former President Bill Clinton.

"Over the last week, I listened to you, and in the process I found my own voice," Clinton told the throng. "Together let's give America the kind of comeback New Hampshire has just given me."

Obama congratulated Clinton on her victory and vowed to keep fighting.

"I'm still fired up and ready to go," he told backers who interrupted him, chanting, "We want change."

The next Democratic stops are Nevada on January 19 and South Carolina a week later. Obama has clear advantages in both states; the powerful Culinary Workers Union reportedly is ready to back him in Nevada, and about half the South Carolina electorate is African-American.

After that, Obama and Clinton will engage in political combat across the country — when organization and money could make a difference — and each candidate has a deep war chest.

The result was less encouraging for Edwards. He drew less than one in five votes, despite having campaigned hard in New Hampshire, including a final 36-hour marathon. Edwards vowed to continue his campaign regardless, hoping to mount a comeback in South Carolina, his native state.

The clash between Obama, who is 46, and Clinton, who is 60, revealed a generation gap and a gender split in New Hampshire voting, exit polls showed.

Voters aged 18-29 went for Obama by a margin of 61 percent to 22 percent. Voters aged 65 and older went for Clinton by 48 percent to 33 percent. There's also a gender gap. Women went for Clinton by 47 percent to 34 percent. Men went for Obama by 42 percent to 30 percent.

— David Lightman and other members of the McClatchy Washington Bureau

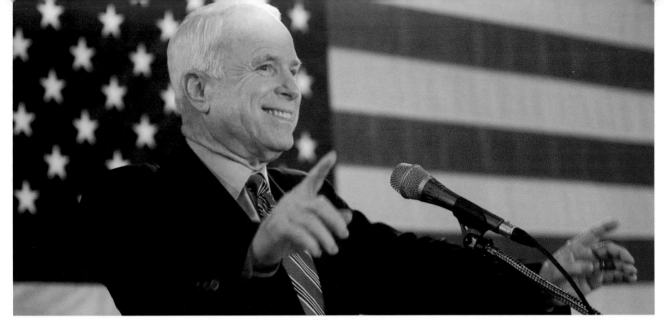

Celebrating his political comeback, John McCain acknowledged cheers from his backers at a hotel in Nashua, New Hampshire. (Darin Oswald/Idaho Statesman/MCT)

In GOP, McCain back on top

Manchester, New Hampshire: January 8, 2008

His campaign all but dead just months ago, John McCain roared back today in the New Hampshire Republican primary. Eight years ago, he launched his bid for the White House with a smashing victory here, and now he hopes to all but knock out Mitt Romney, who governed the state next door until a year ago and has a home here.

As cheering supporters chanted, "Mac is back! Mac is back!," McCain relished his rebound to victory after having been widely counted out when his campaign broke down last summer: "My friends, I'm past the age when I can proclaim myself a kid no matter what adjective precedes it. But tonight we sure showed 'em what a comeback looks like."

McCain pinpointed the beginning of his remarkable comeback — "a very slow snowball," he called it — to a debate just after Labor Day in New Hampshire, when he gave a moving, emotional answer to a young woman who stood to ask whether her brother's death in Iraq had been worth it.

He then embarked on a series of town hall meetings, 101 in all, where he took questions from all comers.

"I've always said I can out-campaign most people," he said. "And with another burst of ego, I can relate to people at a town hall meeting."

— *David Lightman with other members of the McClatchy Washington Bureau*

Clinton takes Nevada

January 19, 2008

Hillary Clinton topped Barack Obama today, 51 to 45 percent, in the Nevada Democratic caucuses. The Democrats now head to South Carolina for their party's primary there in a week.

The Nevada caucus proved to be a classic party struggle between groups that are crucial to any potential nominee. Obama won the backing of the influential Culinary Workers Union, while business interests tended to side with Clinton. Her forces were so concerned about the union's impact that they unsuccessfully went to court to try to stop special caucuses on the Las Vegas Strip where casino and hotel employees could vote.

The state's large Hispanic population was also in play. Latino voters were an estimated 14 percent of Saturday's vote. Clinton got an estimated 64 percent of their vote.

Nevada was the only major Democratic contest between the New Hampshire primary and the South Carolina primary, the party's first Southern contest.

— *David Lightman/ McClatchy Washington Bureau*

Clinton and Obama exchanged remarks as John Edwards listened in a debate sponsored by the Congressional Black Caucus Institute in South Carolina. (Randall Hill/Myrtle Beach Sun News/MCT)

Into the fire

Myrtle Beach, South Carolina: January 21, 2008

Barack Obama and Hillary Clinton broke into bitter verbal warfare tonight, challenging one another's honesty in the most heated debate of their yearlong campaign. Throughout, they stared at one another icily, raised their voices and interrupted one another, all the while repeatedly accusing one another in strikingly personal terms.

"You never take responsibility for any vote," Clinton said at one point, drawing boos from some of the Democrats watching at the Palace Theater.

The jarring clash came as Clinton and Obama grappled for advantage in a close competition — and as their campaigns grew increasingly personal. An added and perhaps aggravating factor: the growing role of former President Bill Clinton attacking Obama, an unprecedented spectacle in a party primary.

Obama noted the challenge — and perhaps the strain — of competing against both Clintons, saying,

"I can't tell who I'm running against sometimes."

He objected to the way the Clintons hammered him for saying recently that Ronald Reagan transformed American politics, insisting he was stating the obvious and not praising Reagan. While he fought Reagan's policies as a community organizer in the poor neighborhoods of Chicago, he said, "you were a corporate lawyer sitting on the board of Wal-Mart."

Clinton countered that she was fighting Reagan while Obama was representing a contributor "in his slum landlord business in inner-city Chicago."

Clinton also worked to turn Obama's complaints against him, suggesting it signaled weakness for a candidate who wants to take on the Republicans.

"I'm used to taking the incoming fire," she said. "But when you get into this arena, you can't expect to have a hands-off attitude about your record."

— Steven Thomma/
McClatchy Washington Bureau

Not enough in Nevada: Despite campaigning hard in events such as this one at the Reno Events Center, Obama came in second in the Nevada caucuses. (Brian Baer/Sacramento Bee/MCT)

'A moment in every generation'

Beaufort, South Carolina: January 24, 2008

Obama supporters filled the bleachers at Battery Creek High School. (F. Brian Ferguson/The Beaufort Gazette)

Ashley Depew, 18, went into today's Barack Obama town hall meeting unsure for whom she would vote, if at all. The Battery Creek High School senior waited an hour and a half to get back into the school and past security checks for the rally this afternoon because Obama had stuck out when she was shopping candidates.

"Usually, I think of presidential candidates as really uptight; they take a really classic approach," said the first time voter-to-be.

She didn't expect the roaring rock-star reception Obama received when he took the stage.

"He's really hip, you could say," Depew said.

It was the candidate's proposed education reforms that won her over. She said his plan to make money for college available to all young people in exchange for volunteer service in homeless shelters, the Peace Corps or other organizations, as well as plans to improve schools and teachers' pay resonated with her.

Obama spoke for about 45 minutes, spending the latter part of his speech quashing rumors about his faith (he is Christian), his willingness to recite the pledge of allegiance (he leads the Senate in it) and cynics' criticism of his trademark message of hope.

"Nothing worthwhile in the nation has ever happened, except for somebody somewhere decided to hope," Obama said. "There's a moment in every generation where that spirit of hope has to come through if we are to make our mark. This is our mark, this is our time."

— Jeremy Hsieh/Beaufort Gazette

Ready to go!

Greenwood, South Carolina: January 24, 2008

Obama shared the stage with Edith Childs of Greenwood. (Gary O'Brien/Charlotte Observer/MCT)

Barack Obama gives passionate campaign speeches, but when it comes to firing up a crowd, he's no Edith S. Childs. Since her days helping organize voting drives and working in South Carolina civil rights efforts, the tiny Childs has been a local legend for being able to bring audiences to their feet — and the polls — with her booming, fiery, cheerleader-style chant of "We're fired up ... Ready to go!"

It became a signature campaign slogan for Obama, thanks to her. Childs, all 5 feet 2 inches of her clad in purple from her church hat to her shoes, had Obama getting funky — or as funky as a United States senator running for president can get — when she joined him on stage at Greenwood's Lander University today and led her chant.

Childs, 59, is an unabashed Obama Girl whom the campaign has adopted and incorporated into the senator's political message — that hope and inspiration can trigger change.

"I'm one of those people who knows how to get people energized," she says. "When you do something like that, it has a domino effect."

— William Douglas/
McClatchy Washington Bureau

Smashing win in South Carolina

Columbia, South Carolina: January 26, 2008

Barack Obama cruised to a decisive victory in South Carolina's presidential primary today with overwhelming support from black voters and about one-fourth of whites as well, a win that leaves Hillary Clinton humbled and John Edwards staggering.

Clinton and her husband, the former president, fought hard in the final days to overtake the Illinois senator, or at least come close in a state where polls found she was the front-runner just last month. Instead, she finished second, with Edwards third. Edwards' showing in his native state, where he won the 2004 primary, is a potentially lethal blow to his already-underdog campaign. Obama won 55 percent of the vote to Clinton's 27 percent. Edwards had 18 percent.

The result sets up a showdown between Obama, and Clinton in 22 states and American Samoa on February 5, when primaries and caucuses will award a total of 1,678 pledged delegates. A candidate needs 2,205 to be nominated.

Clinton tried mightily to create a no-lose scenario in South Carolina, leaving the state in mid-week to visit several February 5 states while her husband, the former president, campaigned full-time in South Carolina. She returned two days ago for a final, frenetic 48 hours of campaigning.

Roughly half the state's voters were black, and many of them came to see the effort by Obama, an African-American, as a movement as much as a campaign. His rallies in the African-American community fired passions rarely seen in politics, and supporters praised him in enthusiastic, even lofty terms.

"Nothing against Clinton, but Obama is making history," said Charlene Thompson, a Columbia purchasing agent.

Clinton's loss is hardly a fatal blow, but it's a setback, particularly among black voters. Many said they were uneasy with anti-Obama comments this month from both Clintons, which they saw as nasty and demeaning.

Obama, Bill Clinton said in one widely noted comment, was engaging in a "the biggest fairy tale that I have ever seen" when describing the history of his Iraq war positions. Hillary Clinton also riled many

Obama proclaimed victory in the South Carolina Democratic primary. (C. Aluka Berry/The State/MCT)

black voters by saying, "Dr. (Martin Luther) King's dream began to be realized when President Johnson passed the Civil Rights Act."

Critics saw that as marginalizing Dr. King and condescending to black activism.

—David Lightman/
McClatchy Washington Bureau

'My brother's keeper'

Macon, Georgia: January 27, 2008

Fresh from big primary victory in South Carolina, Barack Obama came to Macon this morning and delivered not a political message but a largely religious one. He told a church congregation how he became a Christian. Obama is the son of a Kenyan father whom he never really knew and a white woman from Kansas who was "deeply spiritual" but "rebelled from organized religion," he said.

He started going to church as an adult because he wanted Chicago faith leaders to help him organize a job training program. But, in the pew, "I was introduced to Jesus in a way that I had not been introduced before," Obama said.

At the nondenominational, mixed-race Harvest Cathedral Church, each of the 1,100 seats was full, about 400 listened from the lobby and more than 50 members of the media covered the event.

In a sermonlike call to action, Obama mentioned the oft-told biblical story of the Good Samaritan, the man who stopped on the road to Jericho to help a stranger beaten by thieves, even when a priest and Levite who passed by earlier would not.

"Because he stopped, justice was won," Obama said. "I'm talking about the kind of justice ... that rests on the simple precept that I am my brother's keeper, I am my sister's keeper and that our destinies are bound up together."

— *Travis Fain/The Telegraph*

Big endorsement from a big name

Obama stood with Edward Kennedy, right, Rep. Patrick Kennedy and Caroline Kennedy at American University in Washington.
(Chuck Kennedy/MCT)

Washington, D.C.: January 28, 2008

Liberal icon Edward Kennedy endorsed Barack Obama for president today, saying, "I feel change in the air." The endorsement by the veteran Massachusetts Democratic senator came at a pivotal time for Obama, who faces key tests against Hillary Clinton in 22 states on February 5.

Obama won Kennedy's support after the Massachusetts senator became disillusioned with the Clintons' negative campaign tactics in South Carolina. With it, Obama hopes to erode Clinton's hold on longtime Kennedy constituencies, including older Americans, unionized workers and Latinos. Obama told the Kennedys that he felt "a great deal of humility" because "I know what your support means."

— *Margaret Talev/*
McClatchy Washington Bureau

Edwards withdraws from the contest

Washington, D.C.: January 30, 2008

John Edwards quit the presidential campaign today, freeing up blocs of voters who could tip the balance in still-close races. The move could swing votes to both Hillary Clinton and Barack Obama, though probably more to her. Edwards' supporters are similar in demographic profile and outlook to Clinton's. A smaller number were drawn to Edwards

for his outspoken call to change Washington, which could lead them into the Obama camp.

Edwards based his campaign on an outsider promise to change the way Washington does business. He vowed a partisan fight for change while Obama offers a more civil approach, but both are seen less as Washington insiders than Clinton is.

— *Steven Thomma/McClatchy Washington Bureau*

Out West, a state is back in the game...

Boise, Idaho: January 31, 2008

Barack Obama's upcoming visit puts Idaho in a spotlight unseen in at least three decades.

Idaho Democrats used to caucus in March but moved to be part of Super Tuesday, hoping to get some attention. In the past, few candidates of either party came to Idaho. When they did, it was to raise money, typically visiting long before they were needed in battleground states.

The West presents Obama a chance to counter Clinton's strength in Super Tuesday states such as New York, New Jersey and Massachusetts. Idaho, Utah and Colorado are leaning his way, according to various polls.

President Bill Clinton was unpopular in Idaho, and Obama supporters have used that soft spot to organize an ambitious campaign. In Idaho, Obama has campaign offices in Boise, Coeur d'Alene, Idaho Falls, Ketchum and Pocatello; hundreds of volunteers; and 20 paid workers, including vacationing congressional staffers and veterans of Obama campaigns in Iowa and Nevada.

Among the Idaho volunteers are people like Linda Crozier, who was busy Wednesday working on voter turnout efforts at headquarters in Boise. Like many in the Obama camp, she is involved in her first campaign. Word that Obama would actually come to oft-neglected Idaho has energized the campaign still more, Crozier said: "The office has been abuzz. This is the best week yet."

Though Idaho Democrats represent just 23 of the 2,025 delegates required for the nomination, Idaho looks like Obama country. Chani Wiggins, Obama's

As votes were counted in the Idaho caucuses February 5, Obama supporter Tawny Reckamp, left, tried to persuade undecided voter Cathy Hardy to come to the Obama camp. (Joe Jaszewski/Idaho Statesman)

Idaho spokeswoman, said Obama's choosing Idaho shows the race nationwide was close.

"Every delegate matters," she said. "Obama's running a 50-state strategy. He recognizes that red states other candidates fly over are important."

— Dan Popkey/Idaho Statesman

...and engaged

Boise, Idaho: February 2, 2008

Just three days before the Idaho Democratic caucus, Barack Obama spoke to 14,169 people at Taco Bell Arena, a record for the venue and almost triple the nearly 5,000 Democrats who caucused statewide in 2004.

"And they told me there were no Democrats in Idaho," Obama said at the beginning of his 45-minute speech. Many in the audience awoke before dawn and lined up in frigid temperatures to get a seat or stand in the aisles. Even after arena officials opened more seating, they had to turn several thousand more people away.

Clearly aware he was speaking in one of the reddest states in the union, Obama briefly touched on his Christian faith and support for the rights of gun owners, notably hunters. Obama said he has tried to reach out to conservatives and Republicans, citing his ability to work across party lines.

"We can disagree without being disagreeable," he said.

— Anna Webb and Brian Murphy/
Idaho Statesman

Super Tuesday
A big day but no knockout

February 5, 2008

Hillary Clinton today won a string of key battleground states — notably the day's biggest prize, California — with a coalition of women, older voters and moderates, yet Barack Obama nearly matched her with his own series of victories.

Although Obama increasingly had drawn big, enthusiastic crowds across the country, Clinton showed impressive breadth in winning her home state, New York, and the biggest battles, in California, New Jersey, Arizona and Massachusetts, while rolling through Tennessee, Oklahoma and Arkansas.

Obama took primaries in his home state of Illinois and in Missouri, Utah and Connecticut as well as caucuses in North Dakota, Kansas, Minnesota, Idaho, Alaska and Colorado. He also won states with large black voting blocs — Georgia, Alabama and Delaware.

The results mean that the Clinton-Obama duel will continue for weeks.

Clinton's triumph in California was typical of her victories throughout the evening. Fifty-four percent of the voters were women, according to exit polls, and they gave her an 18-point edge. She also beat Obama by 2 to 1 among Latino voters, who made up 29 percent of the electorate, and did well among voters earning less than $50,000 a year.

Obama did well in states such as Georgia, where more than half the voting population was African-American and went for him by 8 to 1. He got 39 percent of whites. His appeal also followed another familiar pattern: He won the 18- to 29-year-old vote by 77 to 21 percent.

While winning statewide popular-vote margins carries psychological importance for any candidate, neither Clinton nor Obama expected to gain a significant advantage from final results in the all-important convention-delegate count because of the Democrats' complex system of awarding delegates.

It takes 2,025 delegates to win the Democratic nomination, and 1,681 were at stake in 22 Super Tuesday contests.

— David Lightman/
McClatchy Washington Bureau

Patti Whiffen, a supporter of Sen. Barack Obama, placed her hand on her heart during the Pledge of Allegiance at the Ada County Democratic caucus at Qwest Arena in Boise, Idaho. (Joe Jaszewski/Idaho Statesman/MCT)

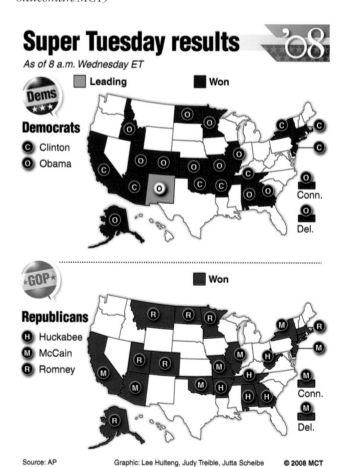

Super Tuesday results '08

As of 8 a.m. Wednesday ET

Leading   Won

Dems

Democrats
C Clinton
O Obama

Conn.

Del.

GOP

Won

Republicans
H Huckabee
M McCain
R Romney

Conn.

Del.

Source: AP   Graphic: Lee Hulteng, Judy Treible, Jutta Scheibe   © 2008 MCT

Impolitic, but will it matter in the long run?

February 20, 2008

Conservative bloggers and talkers were never going to like Barack Obama much anyway. But now their outrage has found a target in the candidate's wife.

Michelle Obama, 44, an Ivy League-educated lawyer (Princeton, Harvard Law), was campaigning for her husband this week in Wisconsin when she said: "For the first time in my adult lifetime, I am really proud of my country. And not just because Barack has done well, but because I think people are hungry for change. And I have been desperate to see our country moving in that direction."

Her impolitic comment immediately hit critical mass on conservative cable TV, talk radio and the Internet. Hillary Clinton's campaign made no comment. But the right's reaction was different.

"I can't keep track of the number of times I've been proud — really proud — of my country since I was born and privileged to live in it," conservative columnist Michelle Malkin said. Rich Galen, another conservative columnist, damned Obama by extensively quoting a conservative favorite, Lee Greenwood's "Proud to be an American." He said America was a place that "gives people like Michelle Obama the right to say excruciatingly stupid things."

And Rush Limbaugh? "Her unhinged comments ring true for many liberals," his Web site's front page said.

Obama tried to revise and extend her remarks today.

"What I was clearly talking about was that I'm proud in how Americans are engaging in the political process," she told WJAR in Providence, Rhode Island. "For the first time in my lifetime, I'm seeing people rolling up their sleeves in a way that I haven't seen and really trying to figure this out, and that's the source of the pride that I was talking about."

Bill Burton, an Obama spokesman, said the right's reaction wasn't a problem for the campaign.

"Just because they're doing it," he said, "doesn't mean there's any sense to it."

The matter is a sort of Rorschach test for what people see in Barack Obama, said James Klumpp, a professor of political communication at the University of Maryland.

"For the Obama people, the explosion of comments ... serves as a confirmation of the critique he is delivering, that this is just the old style of politics that

Michelle Obama in Warwick, Rhode Island, on February 20. (Stephan Savoia/Associated Press)

needs to be changed," Klumpp said. "For those who oppose Obama, it is another kind of confirmation."

And for those voters in the middle, the undecideds and independents who swing elections? Such controversies tend to have short shelf lives, and whether this has any effect on those voters depends largely on what happens next. If the Obamas avoid similar controversies, this probably will be forgotten, Klumpp said.

— *Matt Stearns/McClatchy Washington Bureau*

Obama spoke at Newman Smith High School in Carrollton, Texas, on March 3. (Amy Peterson/Fort Worth Star-Telegram/MCT)

Clinton wins big states, Obama wins delegates — and the fight goes on

March 5, 2008

Weary, divided Democrats looked today toward Pennsylvania's April 22 primary to help sort out the tense, unpredictable struggle being waged by Hillary Clinton and Barack Obama — a fight that seems likely to continue through spring.

Clinton was reveling in having won primaries yeseterday in Texas, Ohio and Rhode Island, launching a comeback for a campaign that even her husband had said could end if she lost Texas and Ohio. But she scored a net gain of only about a dozen convention delegates, leaving her 101 behind Obama. He now has 1,564 delegates to Clinton's 1,463, according to the Associated Press. A total of 2,025 is needed to nominate.

While Obama has the lead, Clinton has the momentum and an argument: that she has prevailed in the big, diverse states the Democratic Party needs to win the White House. That argument could be important if the race ultimately is decided by the 796 party leaders known as superdelegates, who control about 20 percent of the convention's votes.

Superdelegates were created in the early 1980s to balance the sometimes extreme views of party activists with the pragmatic judgment of practical politicians. The goal was to help give the party its best chance to nominate a candidate who could win in November.

While the current superdelegate count favors Clinton, 241 to 202, more than 350 remain undecided.

They're all unpledged; any one of them can switch loyalties at any time.

Clinton suggested that if she won Pennsylvania, the superdelegates should consider the breadth of her vote-getting appeal.

Obama emphasized his own broad appeal.

"We won twice as many states as Senator Clinton," he said. "We have won decisively in a whole number of states, and Senator Clinton and her campaign have tended to cherry-pick states they think are important."

Pennsylvania, with 158 delegates up for grabs on April 22, is the largest of 12 contests remaining. Wyoming holds caucuses in three days, and Mississippi has a primary in a week. Obama is a strong favorite to win both contests, which together have 45 delegates.

After Pennsylvania, the spring calendar includes some states now presumed favorable to Obama, notably North Carolina, Montana, Oregon and South Dakota, while demographics may favor Clinton in Indiana, West Virginia and Kentucky.

Clinton blew Obama an air kiss today when Harry Smith of CBS told her that "a lot of people in Ohio" said they wouldn't mind a Clinton-Obama ticket.

"Well, that may, you know, be where this is headed," she said, laughing.

Later, in a conference call with reporters, her chief strategist, Mark Penn, refused to discuss the possibility, saying the campaign was focused only on winning.

— David Lightman and Margaret Talev/
McClatchy Washington Bureau

McCain ends atop GOP race

March 4, 2008

John McCain has clinched the Republican presidential nomination with a victory in Texas. His win there and in three other states pushed him well over the 1,191 delegates needed for the Republican nomination. It capped a White House campaign that looked all but dead last summer, when he shook up his campaign staff, was short of money and fell behind better-heeled candidates such as former Rudy Giuliani and Mitt Romney.

Mike Huckabee conceded defeat in a speech

to supporters in Irving, Texas, saying he would do "everything possible to unite our party, but more important, to unite our country so that we can be the best that we can be."

"I understand the responsibilities I incur with this nomination," McCain told supporters in Dallas, "and I give you my word, I will not evade or slight a single one. Our campaign must be, and will be, more than another tired debate of false promises, empty sound-bites or useless arguments from the past."

— David Lightman/
McClatchy Washington Bureau

Harsh comments by a longtime minister

Washington, D.C.: March 14, 2008

Barack Obama said today that he would not leave his Chicago church because of incendiary remarks by the pastor, but he condemned the man's controversial statements, which are igniting a firestorm of TV and Internet coverage.

Obama laid out a detailed self-defense of his long, close relationship with the retiring Rev. Jeremiah A. Wright Jr. of the Trinity United Church of Christ in Chicago in a written statement to The Huffington Post, a liberal Web site. Obama also planned a blitz of TV network appearances to counter recent broadcasts of Wright saying "God damn America" and making other inflammatory remarks.

Wright stepped down today from Obama's African American Religious Leadership Committee. In an interview on MSNBC, Obama said that Wright reflected the anger and frustration of an older generation of African-Americans who came of age during the civil rights struggle of the 1960s. He said he did not share that anger because he's a member of a new generation that's enjoyed the benefits accomplished by the earlier generation.

Wright is retiring this year after a long tenure as pastor of the Trinity United Church of Christ in Chicago, whose motto is "unashamedly black and unapologetically Christian." He mentored Obama, performed the Obamas' wedding and informed Obama's 2004 Democratic National Convention speech. His phrase, "the audacity of hope," became the title of Obama's 2006 memoir.

But some of Wright's video-archived sermons deliver harsh messages.

Wright, an African-American, has said that rich whites control the country. He's spoken of the "U.S. of KKK-A." He's compared the World War II atomic bombings of Hiroshima and Nagasaki to the September 11 attacks. He's said that the United States invited the attacks by supporting Israel's treatment of Palestinians.

Obama said that "I ... strongly condemn the statements" from Wright causing controversy. Wright, he said, "has never been my political adviser; he's been my pastor." Obama said that he had never heard Wright make such comments in the church or in private conversations, and that "the sermons I heard him preach always related to our obligation to love God and one another, to work on behalf of the poor and to seek justice at every turn."

— *Margaret Talev/*
McClatchy Washington Bureau

Reverend Jeremiah A. Wright Jr., speaking at a breakfast at the National Press Club in Washington. (Chuck Kennedy/MCT)

An issue we 'cannot afford to ignore'

March 18, 2008

With controversy over his pastor's racially divisive sermons threatening his presidential campaign, Barack Obama tackled race in America head-on today in a speech that drew instant comparisons to John Kennedy's 1960 address about his once-controversial Catholicism.

Speaking in Philadelphia, Obama called slavery America's "original sin" and said mistrust between blacks and whites went both ways. He said racial resentments had long shaped the nation's political landscape but that he thought the country was changing and that he could help heal the divide if elected.

After campaigning for more than a year as an African-American who transcends race rather than lets it define his politics, Obama had no choice but to embrace the subject. Race has surged recently into prominence as a campaign issue, and Democratic voters in some states, especially those with histories of racial division, show increasing signs of voting along racial lines.

"I suppose the politically safe thing would be to move on from this episode and just hope that it fades into the woodwork," Obama said, referring to the firestorm that erupted over racial remarks by his longtime pastor, the Rev. Jeremiah A. Wright Jr. "But race is an issue that I believe this nation cannot afford to ignore right now."

Although he condemns Wright's controversial statements, Obama said, "that isn't all that I know of the man.... He has been like family to me.... I can no more disown him than I can disown the black community."

Nor, Obama said, would he disown his own white grandmother, who loved and helped raise him but "who once confessed her fear of black men who passed by her on the street and who on more than one occasion has uttered racial or ethnic stereotypes that made me cringe."

Obama, whose oratorical gifts lifted him to national prominence, also referred to his rivals, Hillary Clinton and John McCain, in the context of race and the presidential campaign. He noted recent comments by Clinton supporter Geraldine Ferraro, the 1984 Democratic vice presidential candidate, who said that Obama had an unfair advantage because he's black.

"We can pounce on some gaffe by a Hillary supporter as evidence that she's playing the race card, or we can speculate on whether white men will all flock to John McCain in the general election regardless of his policies," Obama said. "Or at this moment, in this election, we can come together and say, 'Not this time.'"

This time, Obama said, America should focus on how to build a more united nation. He said his belief that he could help the country do that is at the core of his candidacy.

The speech was written over the past few days, and Obama stayed up into early this morning polishing it. Obama played "the most significant role" in the writing, a spokeswoman said, with help from his chief speechwriter, Jon Favreau, a white New Englander in his mid-20s, and Obama's chief strategist, David Axelrod, who is Jewish.

Obama said that black men and women of Wright's generation, now in their 60s or older, are still gripped by the humiliation, fear and bitterness of segregation, but he recognizes that "a similar anger exists within segments of the white community. Most working- and-middle-class white Americans don't feel they have been particularly privileged by their race."

They've worked hard and they're threatened by the changing global economy, he acknowledged.

"When they are told to bus their children to a school across town, when they hear that an African-American is getting an advantage in landing a good job or a spot in a good college because of an injustice that they themselves never committed, when they're told that their fears about crime in urban neighborhoods are somehow prejudiced, resentment builds over time."

On both sides of the racial divide, he said, politicians exploited fears.

"It's a racial stalemate we've been stuck in for years," Obama said. "But I have a firm conviction — a conviction rooted in my faith in God and my faith in the American people — that working together, we can move beyond some of our old racial wounds."

But he acknowledged about Wright: "Did I know him to be an occasionally fierce critic of American domestic and foreign policy? Of course. Did I ever hear him make remarks that could be considered controversial while I sat in church? Yes. Did I strongly disagree with many of his political views? Absolutely — just as I'm sure many of you have heard remarks from your pastors, priests or rabbis with which you strongly disagreed."

— Margaret Talev/
McClatchy Washington Bureau

"I love you, too:" Obama at the Grady Cole Center in Charlotte. (Layne Bailey/Charlotte Observer/MCT)

Relaxed candidate, lively audience

Charlotte, North Carolina: March 19, 2008

Speaking to what he called a rowdy crowd here today, Barack Obama pledged to end the war in Iraq and fight special interests, even as he acknowledged that "we're not going to be able to solve all these problems quickly."

A day after delivering a major speech on race and politics in Philadelphia, a relaxed Obama appeared before more than 2,500 people at Grady Cole Center. He was greeted by a deafening ovation and shouts of "We love you, Obama!"

"I love you, too," he replied.

"This is a rowdy crowd," he said at another point, and later urged the boisterous group to "settle down."

The senator spent much of his time amplifying themes from this week's speeches about the war and race.

"The war in Iraq was unwise," he said. "It distracted us from a war that had to be fought against al-Qaida in Afghanistan. I was opposed to it in 2002. I'll bring it to a close in 2009."

One questioner asked Obama about "black-on-black" crime.

"I touched on that a little bit yesterday," he said to a standing ovation, alluding to speech in Philadelphia on race. Part of the problem, he went on, was the history of African-American communities that lacked police, where schools were long segregated, and where federal welfare policies helped foster single-parent homes.

"More and more single moms and fathers not in the picture," he said. One solution is education, he said. Another requires parents to instill values.

"I don't want to make a lot of promises to you I can't keep," he said. "We're not going to be able to solve all of these problems quickly. But the most important thing is, I will wake up every single day thinking about you."

— *Jim Morrill/Charlotte Observer*

On campus, leading cheers

University Park, Pennsylvania: March 31, 2008

Barack Obama delivered a rousing stump speech on Penn State's Old Main lawn today, thrilling a crowd of more than 20,000 people who jammed shoulder to shoulder under a sunny sky and light breeze for a close encounter with the Democratic presidential contest.

Obama's hour-long speech from a stage set amid the sea of supporters capped an 18-hour visit that included an overnight stay at The Penn Stater Conference Center Hotel, a pickup basketball game at the Bryce Jordan Center and an introduction to the College of Agricultural Sciences dairy complex behind Beaver Stadium, where he fed milk to a 1-month-old Holstein. Obama's speech on Old Main lawn pulled in thousands of central Pennsylvanians to mix with thousands of Penn State students.

The crowd was warmed up by songs such as James Brown's "Living in America" blasting through the sound system before introductory remarks by Penn State cornerback Lydell Sargeant and Pennsylvania Sen. Bob Casey.

"We're running as the underdog," Casey said. "Pennsylvanians like underdogs, and Pennsylvanians like a fighter — and that's what we have in Barack Obama. We need a fighter as a president."

"How's it going, Penn State?" Obama called out, and then three times repeated "We are ... !" prompts to "... Penn State!" replies, louder each time. "Look at that crowd! Look at that crowd!" Obama said.

The guts of the speech, familiar to loyal C-SPAN viewers, took up the need to tackle problems such as creating new jobs, establishing universal health care, improving public education and making college affordable. He elicited cheers from the student-dominated crowd when he outlined his plan for a $4,000 tuition credit, to be repaid by a commitment after college to a form of community or national service.

"We'll invest in you, and you must invest in America," he said. He told the crowd that the United States was spending $10 billion a month to fight the Iraq war.

"Imagine if we were spending $10 billion a month in America: building roads, improving schools and laying broadband networks," he said, pledging to roll back President Bush's tax cuts for the wealthiest 1 percent of Americans.

Obama campaign worker Dan Gross said Penn State police estimates put today's crowd at 22,000, but Penn State police said their estimate was 20,000.

The Old Main lawn rally left lasting memories, especially among the young. After Obama's speech, Stevie Wonder's

Obama addressed a crowd on the Old Main lawn at Penn State, top, and fed a calf along with Nadine Houck, assistant manager of the Penn State dairy complex, above. (Christopher Weddle/Centre Daily Times)

"Signed, Sealed, Delivered, I'm Yours" blared out and then Jackie Wilson's "Your Love Keeps Lifting Me" — as Obama and Secret Service agents plunged into the crowd.

Among the hundreds of people the presidential candidate came across was Penn State musical theater major Jonathan Kitt, 22, who got to shake hands with Obama and, afterward, thrilled to the experience.

"I was like: 'You're my hero. I love you. You're great,'" Kitt said. "He was like: 'Thank you.'"

— Mike Joseph/
Centre Daily Times, State College, Pennsylvania

Bitter voters. The Pastor. Ayers. Bosnia

Philadelphia: April 16, 2008

Both Democratic presidential candidates faced questions in debate tonight about the barrage of controversies that have dogged them in recent weeks, from Obama's "bitter" voters comment to Clinton's false claims of coming under sniper fire in Bosnia in 1996.

First came Obama's remarks at an April 6 fundraiser in San Francisco, when he said of small-town voters chronically disappointed at lost jobs and empty promises from Washington: "It's not surprising then they get bitter, they cling to guns or religion or antipathy to people who aren't like them or anti-immigrant sentiment or anti-trade sentiment as a way to explain their frustrations."

Clinton has been bashing Obama over that comment ever since, saying it revealed him to be an out-of-touch elitist. Tonight, she repeated her thrust.

She recalled how her grandfather was a factory worker in Scranton, Pennsylvania.

"I don't believe that my grandfather or my father, or the many people whom I have had the privilege of knowing and meeting across Pennsylvania over many years, cling to religion when Washington is not listening to them," she said. "I similarly don't think that people cling to their traditions, like hunting and guns, either when they are frustrated with the government. I just don't believe that's how people live their lives."

Obama gently tried to cool the furor.

"I think there's no doubt that I can see how people were offended. It's not the first time that I've made, you know, a statement that was mangled up. It's not going to be the last."

Sure, he said, people get frustrated — and are eagerly wooed by politicians vowing to protect their right to worship, or not to take away their guns.

"What is also true is that wedge issues, hot-button issues, end up taking prominence in our politics," Obama explained, "and part of the problem is that when those issues are exploited, we never get to solve the issues that people really have to get some relief on."

As for Obama's relationship with his former pastor, Rev. Jeremiah Wright, Clinton said, "There were so many different variations of the explanations."

Tonight, Obama said that he had known Wright as "somebody who made controversial statements, but they were not of the sort that we saw that offended so many Americans. And that's why I specifically said that these comments were objectionable; they're not comments that I believe in."

Obama's third defense concerned William Ayers, a radical activist who was a member of the Weather Underground, a group that planted bombs. (Three Weather Underground members were killed when a bomb accidentally exploded in 1970, the group's only victims.)

Ayers is on the board of the Woods Fund of Chicago, where Obama also served. Ayers told *The New York Times* seven years ago, "I don't regret setting bombs. I feel we didn't do enough."

Obama was asked to explain his relationship with Ayers, including why he had attended a political event in 1995 at Ayers' home, as reported by Politico.

Obama bristled, saying:

"He's not somebody who I exchange ideas with on a regular basis. And the notion that somehow as a consequence of me knowing somebody who engaged in detestable acts 40 years ago, when I was 8 years old, somehow reflects on me and my values doesn't make much sense."

Clinton was forced to confront her own controversy over her claim last month that she ducked sniper fire in Bosnia 12 years ago, which she did not.

"I may be a lot of things but I'm not dumb," Clinton said. She noted that she'd written accurately about her Bosnia trip in a 2004 memoir, but "on a couple of occasions in past weeks, I said some things I knew weren't the case.... I'm embarrassed by it, I've apologized for it. I've said it was a mistake."

*— David Lightman/
McClatchy Washington Bureau*

Clinton wins, but time's running out

Washington, D.C.: April 22, 2008

Hillary Clinton won a hard-fought Pennsylvania primary today, beating rival Barack Obama in a scrappy victory that she hoped would keep her underdog campaign alive to fight another day.

"Some counted me out and said to drop out," Clinton told cheering supporters in Philadelphia. "But the American people don't quit. And they deserve a president who doesn't quit, either.

"You listened and today you chose.... Because of you, the tide is turning."

In the total delegate count, Obama entered the day leading by 1,648 to 1,509, a margin of 139. Of the 158 delegates up for grabs in Pennsylvania, Clinton won 85 to Obama's 73.

It was her last chance to score a big gain on Obama. Only seven states and Puerto Rico are left to vote, none of them as big.

— Steven Thomma/
McClatchy Washington Bureau

Obama easily takes North Carolina, comes close in Indiana

Raleigh, North Carolina: May 6, 2008

Barack Obama's double-digit victory in North Carolina today and a narrow loss in Indiana brought him closer to clinching the Democratic nomination for president.

Hillary Clinton, meanwhile, said she would continue her fight even as she fell farther behind in the delegate count.

In North Carolina, Obama won a good chunk of its 115 pledged delegates and soared to a solid victory on cascades of support from blacks, young people and voters who say they have been hit hard by the troubled economy. He won 56 percent of the popular vote.

Obama celebrated his victory in the Tar Heel state, speaking to thousands of cheering volunteers and supporters at North Carolina State University's Reynolds Coliseum. He pledged to bring the troubled Democratic party together.

"We cannot give John McCain the chance to serve out George Bush's third term," he said of the presumptive Republican nominee. "We will be united in November."

But Clinton carried almost two-thirds of the white Democratic vote here, and many of those voters told exit pollsters they would not support Obama in November if he's the Democratic nominee.

She also squeaked past Obama in the mostly white, working-class state of Indiana, keeping her presidential hopes alive.

Winded from running up and down the court with the Tar Heel basketball team, Obama benched himself to rest during a workout at the University of North Carolina in Chapel Hill. He was campaigning before the state's primary. (Corey Lowenstein/The News & Observer)

In Indianapolis, Clinton said she would now move to other primary states where, she said, "their voices have not been heard for far too long."

"I'm running to be the president of all America -- north, south, east, west," she said.

— Barbara Barrett/
The News & Observer, Raleigh, North Carolina

The nominee
Marathon primaries end with Obama No. 1

Washington, D.C.: June 3, 2008

Barack Obama clinched the Democratic presidential nomination tonight, seizing a place in American history on the final day of a grueling five-month primary that forced him to battle rival Hillary Clinton to the very end.

The 46-year-old senator from Illinois became the first African-American to win a major political party presidential nomination and lead it into a general election. He'll face John McCain, 71, at a time when Americans are anxious about the economy at home and wars in Iraq and Afghanistan.

Clinton, who kept her long-shot hopes alive for months with late primary wins, appeared to bow to the inevitable.

"It has been an honor to contest these primaries with him just as it is an honor to call him my friend," she told supporters in New York.

Obama wrapped up a majority of delegates needed to win the nomination at the party's August convention in Denver as a tide of unelected super delegates came out for him throughout the day. The Associated Press declared that Obama had clinched the nomination even before the final two primaries in Montana and South Dakota were finished, saying he had surpassed the 2,118 delegates needed. CNN and NBC declared him over the top soon after the South Dakota polls closed. Clinton won South Dakota and Obama took Montana. Both victories were incidental to the delegate count.

A flood of more than 26 superdelegates, among them former President Jimmy Carter, added their names to the roll minutes after the last polls closed.

"Sixteen months have passed since we first stood together on the steps of the Old State Capitol in Springfield, Illinois," Obama said. "Thousands of miles have been traveled. Millions of voices have been heard. Tonight, we mark the end of one historic journey with the beginning of another — a journey that will bring a new and better day to America.

"Tonight, I can stand here and say that I will be the Democratic nominee for president of the United States of America," he said to thunderous applause from supporters in St. Paul, Minnesota. Minnesota will be the site of September's Republican National Convention.

He praised Clinton, lauding her as "a leader who inspires millions with her strength" and said she would play a role in the promised accomplishments of an Obama presidency.

Turning to McCain, he saluted the veteran's life of public service but insisted that they had very different agendas:

"My differences with him are not personal; they are with the policies he has proposed in this campaign."

He criticized McCain for standing too often with President Bush, supporting economic policies he said had hurt American jobs and paychecks, and for maintaining support for the Iraq war.

"We must be as careful getting out of Iraq as we

> Thus ended the longest and costliest primary campaign in U.S. history: more than 16 months of fulltime campaigning since Obama and Clinton declared their candidacies.

were careless getting in — but start leaving we must," Obama said.

McCain, in Kenner, Louisiana, said, "The general election campaign has begun."

He, too, vowed to change the country's course, but said Obama offered the wrong course on Iraq and on the promise of government help for economic woes.

Thus ended the longest and costliest primary campaign in U.S. history: more than 16 months of fulltime campaigning since Obama and Clinton declared their candidacies, five months of voting in 54 contests and more than half a billion dollars raised and spent by Obama and the rest of the Democratic field.

— Steven Thomma with William Douglas, Margaret Talev and David Lightman/ McClatchy Washington Bureau

---

The many faces of Obama: At Nissan Pavilion in Bristow, Virginia, after clinching the nomination. (Chuck Kennedy/MCT)

How the Obama team did it

Washington, D.C.: June 3, 2008

How did Barack Obama upset Hillary Clinton for the Democratic presidential nomination? Was it because:

A.) He worked harder in Iowa and other caucus and early-voting states and built a national movement of youth and grass-roots activists and small-dollar donors?

B.) His campaign staff worked more harmoniously than Clinton's and without a sense of entitlement?

C.) His string of victories after the February 5 Super Tuesday contests cost Clinton so much in delegates, momentum and money that her big wins later on weren't enough?

D.) He's a gifted speechmaker whose message of change and less divisive politics had broader appeal than Clinton's claim that she was ready on day one?

Answer: All of the above.

With the last primaries over and the general election ahead, Obama, his advisers and thousands of volunteers are looking back proudly on what political science professors will teach for years as a new model for how to campaign for president.

"Hillary, before Super Tuesday, thought it was going to end on Super Tuesday, but the Obama campaign kept winning in the caucus states," said Roy Romer, a former Colorado governor and a Democratic National Committee chairman during Bill Clinton's presidency. Romer endorsed Obama in mid-May.

"He tapped into an urge of many people to participate, and he gave them a means of participating, and kept them informed through an e-mail network, and he got them feeling they were part of the campaign and making history happen. And he had a personal charisma that struck a chord deeply in the American psyche."

"We took them by storm!" recalled Matt Robb, 23, a student at Michigan State University who spent eight months in Iowa as an unpaid intern for the Obama campaign and later as a paid organizer.

Robb spent hours every day making phone calls, breaking down surveys on Iowans' sentiments and building databases of the results. He marveled at the intricacy of one of the Obama campaign's strategies, to enlist high school students old enough to caucus in the hope that they'd also sway their parents to the candidate.

Behind the new faces, however, was a team of battle-tested advisers, many of whom had worked for former presidential hopefuls and Democratic leaders such as Dick Gephardt, Tom Daschle, John Kerry, John Edwards, Howard Dean, Joseph Lieberman — and the Clintons.

Obama's chief strategist, David Axelrod, also previously worked with other high-level African-American candidates who needed to appeal to white audiences. Campaign manager David Plouffe, a partner in Axelrod's Chicago-based consulting firm, oversaw the strategy that emphasized winning Iowa and racking up pledged delegates in places where Clinton wasn't competing over concentrating on big states and the popular vote.

Obama brought his own experiences to the table.

"He started out as a community organizer, so he recognized the power of a grass-roots campaign," said Valerie Jarrett, a Chicago businesswoman, a senior adviser to the campaign and a close friend of the Obamas. "There are far more people involved in this campaign from volunteers to small-dollar donors than we've seen in the history of politics before.

"Barack and David Plouffe deserve a great deal of credit for focusing on Iowa when there was a lot of pressure to broaden his strategy to a national strategy. Donors were saying, 'We've been supportive, why are you still lagging in the national polls?'" But Obama and Plouffe maintained that "if he could win Iowa, it would generate enthusiasm and confidence throughout the rest of the country."

Obama won Iowa, lost New Hampshire, took South Carolina by storm, held his own on Super Tuesday, then enjoyed a winning streak that included white general-election battleground states such as Wisconsin and Virginia.

Clinton replaced campaign managers and strategists, dug in and won in important places such as Ohio, Pennsylvania and West Virginia. But by then, many of the party's superdelegates, who ultimately decided the close contest, already had come to think that it was over, and that Obama had earned the nomination.

— Margaret Talev/
McClatchy Washington Bureau

Now the presumptive Democratic nominee, Obama worked the handshake line at a rally in Virginia.
(Chuck Kennedy/MCT)

Hello, world: As part of an international tour in July, Obama spoke to tens of thousands of people at the Victory Column in Berlin.(Jae C. Hong/Associated Press)

'Our moment,' Obama tells Germans

Berlin, Germany: July 24, 2008

In a highly unusual move for an American presidential candidate, Barack Obama staged a foreign policy speech today before a huge overseas audience, implicitly criticizing President Bush and calling for transatlantic cooperation to rein in Iran, fight religious extremism and terrorism, and address global warming and poverty.

"People of Berlin, people of the world, this is our moment, this is our time," Obama told an enthusiastic outdoor crowd, which local authorities estimated at more than 200,000. "I know my country has not perfected itself. We've made our share of mistakes and there are times when our actions around the world have not lived up to our best intentions."

The Europeans roared with approval.

Speaking before sunset at the Victory Column in Berlin's Tiergarten, to a crowd that stretched close to a mile back to the Brandenburg Gate, Obama recalled the celebration after the 1989 fall of the Berlin Wall. He warned that today "the greatest danger of all is to allow new walls to divide us from one another."

"In Europe, the view that America is part of what has gone wrong in our world, rather than a force to help make it right, has become all too common," he said. "In America, there are voices that deride and deny the importance of Europe's role in our security and our future. Both views miss the truth."

Obama arrived in Germany this morning to much fanfare. Local television stations aired live coverage and fans gathered in the streets for a glimpse of him outside his hotel and as he arrived for a meeting with Chancellor Angela Merkel.

Before leaving Israel for Germany, Obama visited the Western Wall in Jerusalem, accompanied by a rabbi. Obama slipped a prayer note between one of the gaps in the stone, as is customary, placed a hand on the wall and bowed his head.

—*Margaret Talev/McClatchy Washington Bureau*

For running mate, it's Biden

Springfield, Illinois: August 23, 2008

Sen. Joe Biden of Delaware took on the role of Barack Obama's presidential running mate today, making clear that whatever doubts he had previously expressed about Obama's readiness were gone.

In a joint appearance, Biden called Obama an inspiration to millions with "steel in his spine" and "a clear-eyed pragmatist who will get the job done."

He went after John McCain, a longtime personal friend, as having given "into the right wing of his party and yielded to the very Swift Boat politics he once so deplored."

He also said McCain was so wealthy and insulated from average people's concerns that his version of making difficult kitchen-table decisions was that "he'll have to figure out which of his seven kitchen tables to sit at."

The appearance culminated a frenetic week of speculation over who would get the nod from Obama. In the end, it was a long-time Washington figure whose Roman Catholic faith and blue-collar credentials seemed intended to shore up Obama's electoral weak spots.

Obama introduced the 65-year-old Biden before a crowd estimated at 35,000 outside the Illinois Old

A smiling Biden. (Brian Baer/Sacramento Bee/MCT)

State Capitol. Obama's campaign promised supporters that they would be the first to know if they signed up to receive text messages. But Biden's selection leaked late last night, hours before the text message went out. Then, technical glitches meant some who signed up received their messages late or not at all.

— *Margaret Talev/*
McClatchy Washington Bureau

Clinton on Obama's side, now

Fresno, California: August 24, 2008

On the eve of the Democratic National Convention, Hillary Clinton came here today to thank the United Farm Workers for supporting her campaign for president and to ask that they now turn that support toward electing Barack Obama.

Speaking to a crowd of about 600 people at the union's constitutional convention downtown, Clinton also pledged to continue pressing for immigration reform in Congress, including a provision that would give more than a million undocumented workers in the country a path toward citizenship.

"I stood up for you because I know America can do better," Clinton told members of the union that endorsed her in February's California Democratic

presidential primary. She said the union's work had helped make visible the plight of some of the country's lowest-paid workers.

The last time Clinton made a campaign stop in Fresno, last October, she was stumping for her own candidacy for president. Today, speaking before a crowd that cheered for her as they held up "Obama '08" placards, Clinton praised the man to whom she conceded her party's nomination in June as a politician who also would fight for the union's causes.

"I've seen his passion and determination, his grit and grace, and I know that he has lived the American dream," she said. Clinton added that an Obama presidency would lead to stronger union rights, immigration reform, an increased minimum wage and "a health-care system that takes care of everyone."

— *Jeff St. John/The Fresno Bee*

Democratic convention
The Barack Obama she knows

Denver: August 25, 2008

Michelle Obama introduced Barack Obama to a national audience tonight as a loving husband and father and a dedicated public servant who shared the same values as other working-class Americans.

The wife of the presumptive Democratic presidential nominee was the closing speaker on the opening night of the Democratic National Convention, a moment designed to show the couple's softer side and to take control of a personal narrative that Obama's Republican rival is trying to frame.

"I come here tonight as a sister, blessed with a brother who is my mentor, my protector and my

> ## "I come here as a wife who loves my husband and believes he will be an extraordinary president."

lifelong friend," she told a prime-time television audience and conventioneers gathered here. "I come here as a wife who loves my husband and believes he will be an extraordinary president."

After his wife spoke, a beaming Barack Obama told the Denver convention via video conference from a family's home in Kansas City: "Now you know why I asked her out so many times, even though she said no. You want a persistent president."

In addressing the convention, Michelle Obama reprised her crucial role during the Democratic presidential primaries as deal-closer. It was Michelle Obama who, early in the campaign, visited black beauty salons and black college campuses to tell skeptical African-American voters that her husband was "black enough" and seasoned enough to be president.

Tonight's appearance — which included a biographical video featuring her mother and older brother — was a high-stakes effort to counter Internet rumors and conservative talk-radio suggestions that Barack Obama isn't American or patriotic enough to be president and that she had a hidden left-wing political agenda. Her message to the country: We're just as American as you.

"Barack and I were raised with so many of the same values: that you work hard for what you want in life; that your word is your bond and you do what you say you're going to do; that you treat people with dignity and respect, even if you don't know them, and even if you don't agree with them," she said. "And Barack and I set out to build lives guided by these values, and pass them on to the next generation."

Michelle Obama has been an active player in her husband's campaign, and his foes have tried to tag her as unpatriotic or angry. Critics pounced on her last February when she told an audience that "for the first time in my adult lifetime I am really proud of my country." A Fox News Channel video scroll referred to her as Obama's "baby mama" and a Fox commentator called a seemingly playful fist bump between Michelle and Barack Obama a "terrorist fist jab."

A 44-year-old hospital executive and mother of two, Obama described herself as a daughter of Chicago's South Side, raised by a loving family in a one-bedroom apartment in a brick bungalow. Her mother, Miriam Robinson, was a stay-at-home mom. Her father, Fraser, worked for the city's water department, despite combating multiple sclerosis. Both parents instilled in their two children a drive to succeed.

Michelle met Barack Obama in 1989 when the Chicago law firm she was working for assigned her to mentor the-then summer associate from Harvard. They were married three years later. Michelle Obama is the vice president for community and external affairs for the University of Chicago Medical Center, though she's been on leave since January to help with her husband's campaign.

— William Douglas/
McClatchy Washington Bureau

High ideals in the high country

Denver: August 28, 2008

On a historic occasion echoing the dreams of Dr. Martin Luther King Jr. and John F. Kennedy, Barack Obama tonight became the first African-American to accept a major-party presidential nomination.

His 42-minute speech, delivered softly and seriously at one moment and reaching for lofty heights at another, was steeped in historic allusions: The address at Invesco Field at Mile High stadium echoed John Kennedy, who was the last person to accept his party's nomination in an outdoor sports stadium. Kennedy pledged in 1961 to put an American on the moon by the end of the decade, a goal that was met.

Obama's speech also came 45 years to the day after King gave his "I Have a Dream" speech at the Lincoln Memorial in Washington, a historic oration that laid the spiritual foundation for the civil rights movement that Obama arguably culminates.

"It is that promise that 45 years ago today brought Americans from every corner of this land to stand together on a Mall in Washington, before Lincoln's memorial, and hear a young preacher from Georgia speak of his dream," Obama said.

What people heard that day, he said, was that "in America, our destiny is inextricably linked. That together, our dreams can be one." As he spoke, his voice rose, the crowd stood and thousands waved American flags.

Obama's address came a day after the 100th birthday of former President Lyndon B. Johnson, who signed two major civil-rights laws in the mid-1960s that also helped pave the way for Obama's ascendance. LBJ was remembered at the Democratic convention in a video tribute.

Obama addressed a packed stadium in which people had been waiting up to seven hours for his address.

Obama's speech sought to achieve four goals: to make his life story familiar to Americans, to spell out specifics of what he hopes to achieve, to challenge presumptive Republican presidential nominee John McCain and to assure Americans that the Illinois senator has a foreign-policy vision and a grasp of national security imperatives.

He was introduced with a video about his life, a "childhood like any other," the narrator said. In his address, Obama talked about his mother, "who raised my sister and me on her own while she worked and earned her degree, who once turned to food stamps." And he talked of his grandfather who "marched in Patton's Army and was rewarded by a grateful nation with the chance to go to college on the GI Bill."

The people who served, Obama said as his voice rose, "have not served a red America or a blue America. They have served the United States of America." It was his most popular line, as people stood, roared and waved their flags.

As an estimated 84,000 people jammed the football stadium, Obama turned to the themes he's expected to emphasize throughout the fall campaign.

He tied McCain squarely to President Bush. The

"We are the party of Roosevelt. We are the party of Kennedy."

record is clear, he said: "John McCain has voted with George Bush 90 percent of the time. Senator McCain likes to talk about judgment, but really, what does it say about your judgment when you think George Bush was right more than 90 percent of the time?"

He took on critics who say that McCain, a Vietnam veteran and four-term senator, is better equipped to handle national security.

"We are the party of Roosevelt. We are the party of Kennedy. So don't tell me that Democrats won't defend this country," Obama said. "Don't tell me that Democrats won't keep us safe. The Bush-McCain foreign policy has squandered the legacy that generations of Americans — Democrats and Republicans — have built, and we are here to restore that legacy."

— *David Lightman with Jessica Cherry/*
McClatchy Washington Bureau

A stadium full of delegates and fans hailed Obama on the last night of the Democratic National Convention at Invesco Field at Mile High in Denver. (Andrews/Kennedy/MCT)

From the far North, a running mate

Dayton, Ohio: August 29, 2008

John McCain today chose Sarah Palin, the governor of Alaska, as his candidate for vice president. Palin, 44, is a first-term governor known for being a maverick who's willing to challenge her own party, a key trait that McCain hopes will help him attract independent voters. She has been called a reformer within a state Republican Party that has been rocked by scandal, credentials that may enhance McCain's similar image.

Palin is an abortion rights opponent who's also popular with social conservatives, a key Republican constituency. Her gender could help McCain steal away some women who supported Hillary Clinton in the Democratic primaries but were angry that she wasn't chosen as Barack Obama's running mate. While the rift between Clinton supporters and those who backed Obama appeared to be largely healed at the Democratic National Convention, recent polls have shown that nearly 50 percent of Clinton supporters across the country remain uncommitted to Obama.

Palin's lack of experience in foreign policy and national security could raise concerns, especially because Republicans have made that a key point of attack against Obama. With McCain turning 72 today, his bid to put a 44-year-old first-term governor without national-security credentials a heartbeat away from the presidency is certain to become an issue this fall.

— *William Douglas and Steven Thomma/*
McClatchy Washington Bureau

Palin at an interview in her downtown Anchorage office in summer 2007. The bearskin rug on the sofa was a grizzly shot in the Denali Highway country by her father. (Stephen Nowers/Anchorage Daily News)

McCain and Palin acknowledge delegates after McCain's acceptance speech to the Republican National Convention in St. Paul, Minnesota. (Brian Baer/Sacramento Bee/MCT)

GOP ticket energized by its No. 2

St. Paul, Minnesota: September 4, 2008

The Republicans will emerge from their national convention with a new star — and it isn't their presidential nominee. It's vice-presidential candidate Sarah Palin.

Even with John McCain's speech this evening, it was clear that he will share the spotlight through the fall with his charismatic No. 2 rather than watch her slip into the shadows, as running mates normally do. It's even possible that he may slip into her shadow. Either way, McCain appeared confident sharing the starring role as he claimed the nomination.

"I'm very proud to have introduced our next vice president to the country," he told the convention tonight. "But I can't wait until I introduce her to Washington. And let me offer an advance warning to the old, big-spending, do-nothing, me-first, country-second Washington crowd: Change is coming."

Palin's higher-than-normal profile could have a downside if the one-term Alaska governor strikes swing voters as too strident, as Democrats said today, or too inexperienced, as they've said all week. But the upside was clear immediately.

Her strong performance speaking to the convention last night excited the party's conservative base and gave Republican insiders hoped for the first time that they could get volunteers to knock on doors and battle street by street, a critical tool in a close election.

Palin instantly appealed to contributors. McCain's once lackluster fundraising jumped by $10 million in the days after he picked her.

"A lot of people can give a good speech," said Vin Weber, a former Republican congressman from Minnesota and top party strategist. "Only occasionally is there someone who also connects with people in a very personal way. She connected. She has that X factor."

— Steven Thomma/McClatchy Washington Bureau with Lindsey Lanzendorfer and Natasha Ludwig

THE HOME STRETCH

An estimated 100,000 people gathered in St. Louis between the Old Courthouse and the Gateway Arch to hear Barack Obama on October 18. They represented his biggest crowd to that point in the fall campaign. (Derik Holtmann/Belleville News-Democrat)

As campaign kicks off, McCain, Obama in dead heat

Washington, D.C.: September 11, 2008

John McCain and Barack Obama head into the race for the presidency neck and neck, according to a new Ipsos/McClatchy poll. The national poll finds McCain with the support of 46 percent of registered voters and Obama with 45 percent. The survey has a margin of error of plus or minus 3.3 percentage points.

Independent candidate Ralph Nader has 2 percent and Libertarian candidate Bob Barr 1 percent. Six percent were undecided or didn't support any of those choices.

"McCain got a very good bump from his convention and now it's a real race," said Clifford Young, senior vice president of Ipsos Public Affairs. The poll was conducted September 5-9, the first by Ipsos since the two major-party conventions kicked off the fall general election campaign.

With the Obama-McCain race so close less than two months before the election, several factors could prove pivotal in coming weeks, including how the two campaigns do in winning the support of the roughly 15 percent of voters who could go either way, and how well Republican vice presidential nominee Sarah Palin does in assuring skeptics that she's up to the job. The poll finds that registered voters continue to wonder whether Palin, a first-term Alaska governor, is as qualified to become president as her Democratic counterpart, Joseph Biden, who has been in the Senate more than three decades.

A majority of voters, 60 percent, think that Biden is qualified to be president; 31 percent think he is not. By comparison, 48 percent of voters think Palin is qualified and 44 percent think she is not.

"While Palin has electrified the base, her overall appeal is less than Biden's," Young said.

On issues, McCain leads on foreign policy and national security. Obama leads on jobs and the economy, health care and representing change.

Voters split almost evenly on which is a better leader. "Neither has been able to dominate on that," Young said.

— Steven Thomma/
McClatchy Washington Bureau

Markets fall and candidates push for regulation

Washington, D.C.: September 15, 2008

The Democratic and Republican presidential candidates reacted to today's stock market plunge by calling for more federal regulation and criticizing Wall Street, the Bush administration — and one another.

John McCain, campaigning in Florida, initially sought to calm investors, saying, "I think, still, the fundamentals of our economy are strong." But he soon sounded a harsher tone against his own party, saying that Lehman Brothers' bankruptcy, the cheap sale of Merrill Lynch and reverberations on Wall Street were "a failure of government" and "a failure of regulatory agencies."

Barack Obama, campaigning in Colorado, said that although he didn't fault McCain personally for the financial crisis, "I do fault the economic philosophy he subscribes to." Obama said that President Bush and his Republican Party had insufficiently regulated the lending industry and put too much emphasis on protecting the fortunes of the wealthy.

"Instead of prosperity trickling down, the pain has trickled up," Obama said.

McCain pledged that, along with running mate Sarah Palin, "We will never put America in this position again. We will clean up Wall Street." He did not offer much detail.

"Regulators have been asleep at the switch," McCain said, "and we've got to fix it."

In an e-mail, McCain campaign officials provided a broad outline of McCain's plan, which includes strengthening disclosure in the lending process so borrowers know exactly what they are getting into and complete disclosure of all cash and non-cash compensation of corporate CEOs.

Obama proposed a six-point plan in March to reform the regulatory system. His plan includes giving the Federal Reserve basic supervisory authority over institutions to which it might later be asked to extend credit. Also, he would strengthen capital and disclosure requirements for financial institutions and investigate rating agencies.

— Margaret Talev and William Douglas/
McClatchy Washington Bureau

McCain and Sen. Lyndsey Graham, to his left, walked through the Capitol between meetings among Republican leaders in Washington. (Chuck Kennedy/MCT)

McCain seeks to delay first debate amid deepening financial crisis

Washington, D.C.: September 24, 2008

John McCain shook up the presidential campaign today, announcing that he had suspended campaigning to work on the Wall Street bailout legislation and urging that the first presidential debate with rival Barack Obama be delayed. Obama rejected that proposal and said he still planned to attend the debate in Mississippi. Debate sponsors also said it would go on as planned even if McCain's attendance was in doubt.

McCain's surprise move, coming two days before the first of three long-scheduled presidential debates, offered him a high-risk chance to reshuffle the political deck heading into the final five weeks of the campaign. An aide said that McCain also would suspend television advertising and fundraising.

Obama said the Wall Street crisis underscored the need for the candidates to explain what they would do as president.

"This is exactly the time when the American people need to hear from the person who, in approximately 40 days, will be responsible for dealing with this mess," he told reporters in Clearwater, Florida, where he was preparing for the debate. It's scheduled to focus on foreign policy and national security.

Obama also took a veiled swipe at McCain for the implication that the candidates could only handle one thing at a time.

"Presidents are going to have to deal with more than one thing at a time," he said. "It's not necessary for us to think that we can only do one thing and suspend everything else."

— *Steven Thomma/*
McClatchy Washington Bureau and Beth
Reinhard/The Miami Herald

Obama and McCain addressed a question at the University of Mississippi in Oxford. (Chip Somodevilla, pool/Associated Press)

Debate, on schedule, covers fiscal woes

Oxford, Mississippi: September 26, 2008

Against the backdrop of growing national fears about the U.S. economy, John McCain and Barack Obama sparred tonight over fiscal and foreign policy in their first presidential debate. Organizers stuck with their schedule despite McCain's call to delay it.

Obama painted McCain as a disciple of what he called the failed economic policies of President Bush, which he believed didn't include enough regulation. McCain characterized Obama as pandering for hundreds of millions of dollars in earmarks, only decrying the practice after he decided to run for president. Obama argued that McCain wanted to cut taxes for what he termed some of the wealthiest corporations, costing the Treasury $300 billion. That's small, he said, compared to the roughly $18 billion that earmarks cost each year.

Moderator Jim Lehrer also quizzed the candidates about the keys to success in Iraq and Afghanistan. McCain accused Obama of taking a defeatist attitude in Iraq and calling for a troop withdrawal before the job was done. Once troop levels increased, he said, the situation improved.

"This strategy has succeeded and we are winning in Iraq," McCain said.

Obama asserted the war was badly bungled and shouldn't have been started until the situation in Afghanistan was under control.

"We've spent over $600 billion so far, soon to be $1 trillion," Obama said. "We have lost over 4,000 lives. We have seen 30,000 wounded, and most importantly from a strategic national security perspective, al-Qaida is resurgent, stronger now than at any time since 2001."

But McCain said Obama has taken an exit strategy for Iraq that many of the top decision makers in the military deemed dangerous.

— *Michael Newsom/ Biloxi Sun-Herald*

Palin stands toe-to-toe with Biden, but the contest appears unchanged

Washington, D.C.: October 3, 2008

Sarah Palin gave as good as she got, but will it be enough? The first-term Alaska governor, a Republican, gave a sharper performance in her 90-minute debate with Democratic vice presidential rival Joe Biden last night than she had in recent TV interviews, which have drawn comedy show ridicule, scorn from some fellow conservatives and a dramatic drop in trust from voters.

But she didn't score the kind of dramatic breakthrough that she did when she burst onto the national stage with a strong, in-your-face speech at the Republican National Convention. This time, her opponent was there to answer back, and he argued his case forcefully as well.

Ultimately, both candidates played to their strengths — she the plain-talking hockey mom with a familiar language and style, and he the veteran insider with a fluency in policy, but also a common touch.

Each worked to shore up weaknesses. She did it by talking with readiness, if not ease, on subjects ranging from health care tax credits to a two-state solution to the Israeli-Palestinian conflict. He did it by striving, not always successfully, to avoid talking down to people.

For Palin, the stakes were enormous as the McCain-Palin ticket falls behind in polls, both nationally and in many battleground states. Just hours before the debate, the McCain-Palin campaign said it would shift money and staff out of the battleground state of Michigan, a state they had hoped to take back from the Democrats.

She went on the attack early and often, accusing the Obama-Biden ticket of naivete in foreign policy and tax-and-spend policies domestically, which she said would cost jobs and hurt the economy. She also spoke in the folksy style that underscored her distance, geographically and stylistically, from Washington.

"Say it ain't so," she said to Biden at one point.

To illustrate a point about the impacts of the Wall Street mess, she urged listeners to "go to a kids' soccer game on Saturday and turn to any parent on the sideline, and I bet you you're going to hear fear in that parent's voice."

Asked to say what promises she might have to break because of the Wall Street mess at another point, she winked and said, "How long have I been at this, like five weeks? So there hasn't been a whole lot that I've promised, except to do what is right for the American people."

It delighted some conservatives who had grown anxious about her performance. She also appeared better versed in policy than she had in some of the TV interviews. But she often appeared eager to move past one subject to another where she felt more comfortable.

Pressed by moderator Gwen Ifill to respond to a Biden point on bankruptcy regulations, she said, "That is not so, but because that's just a quick answer, I want to talk about, again, my record on energy versus your ticket's energy ticket, also."

Biden approached the debate carefully, addressing Palin formally as "the governor" while referring to others by their first names, a familiar "John" for McCain, "Gwen" for moderator Gwen Ifill.

— Steven Thomma/McClatchy Washington Bureau

Joe Biden and Sarah Palin shook hands before the start of the vice presidential debate at Washington University in St. Louis. (Jeff Roberson/ Associated Press)

Economy, doubts about Palin help Democrats

October 7, 2008

Barack Obama has opened a 7-point lead over John McCain, according to a new Ipsos/McClatchy poll. It's the biggest so far and appears to come from two key factors:

First, voters are ever more anxious about the faltering economy and trust Obama by a 15-point margin over McCain to steer it.

Second, their confidence that McCain's running mate, Sarah Palin, is qualified to step into the presidency if necessary has fallen sharply.

Obama had the support of 47 percent of registered voters and McCain 40 percent.

With less than a month before Election Day, 9 percent remained undecided or uncommitted, and nearly one in 10 supporters of the two top candidates said they still could change their minds. The poll of

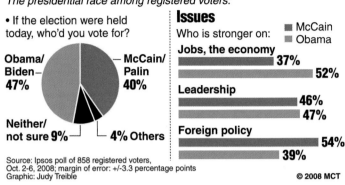

Ipsos-McClatchy Poll

Obama gains

The presidential race among registered voters:

- If the election were held today, who'd you vote for?

Obama/Biden— 47%
McCain/Palin 40%
Neither/not sure 9%
4% Others

Issues
Who is stronger on:
■ McCain
■ Obama

Jobs, the economy — 37% / 52%
Leadership — 46% / 47%
Foreign policy — 54% / 39%

Source: Ipsos poll of 858 registered voters, Oct. 2-6, 2008; margin of error: +/-3.3 percentage points
Graphic: Judy Treible

© 2008 MCT

858 registered voters was taken October 2-6.

— *Steven Thomma/McClatchy Washington Bureau*

Palin's Florida mission: Keep the base enthusiastic, engaged

Miami: October 7, 2008

Sarah Palin's itinerary in Florida, where she went on the offensive over Barack Obama's ties to Vietnam-era radical William Ayers, suggested her mission was to drive the Republican faithful to the polls, rather than to win new converts to the McCain-Palin ticket. Three of her four public appearances over the last two days were in Republican strongholds in southwest and northern Florida.

In the midst of her public appearances, Palin was slated to attend private fundraisers in Naples, Boca Raton and Jacksonville expected to raise as much as $3 million.

Palin showed she could generate a crowd among the faithful. An appearance that was originally scheduled for Fort Myers was moved to a nearby minor-league hockey arena in Estero to accommodate the demand for tickets. At the hockey arena, Palin portrayed Obama as a left-wing zealot with ties to Ayers.

"Wait a minute. He didn't know that he had launched his political career in the living room of a domestic terrorist?" Palin asked the amped-up crowd of 8,000. "This is about the truthfulness and judgment needed in our next president."

Obama's camp said she was exaggerating his relationship with Ayers and hit back with a Web video tying McCain to Charles Keating, the banker at the center of the savings and loan crisis of the 1980s.

Palin also argued that McCain would set the economy straight, while Obama would raise taxes, and she accused Obama of trying to cut off funding to the troops in Iraq and demeaning the military mission in Afghanistan, charges that are echoed in a new McCain ad airing on national cable.

"It sure would be nice if just once (Obama) said he wants America to win," Palin said.

—*Beth Reinhard/Miami Herald*

Palin waved to supporters at Clearwater's Coachman Park in her "Road to Victory" rally in Clearwater, Florida. (Tiffany Tompkins-Condie/Bradenton Herald/MCT)

How to fix financial crisis: Candidates offer competing ideas in second debate

Nashville: October 7, 2008

Reaching out to an anxious nation, John McCain and Barack Obama vied in a spirited debate tonight over who would be the better steward of an economy in crisis.

"Americans are angry, they're upset, and they're a little fearful," McCain said at the outset of the pressure-packed event. "It's our job to fix the problem."

"You need somebody in Washington working for you," Obama said.

With stock markets plummeting, the economy dominated questions posed by voters both inside the town hall style session and over the Internet. Participants in the 90-minute meeting were 80 undecided voters from the Nashville area selected by the Gallup polling organization. The debate, held at Belmont University, was moderated by NBC's Tom Brokaw.

McCain said he would shore up the economy by keeping taxes low, pushing energy independence and ordering the Treasury Department to buy up bad mortgages to stabilize home values.

"It's my proposal," he said. "It's not Sen. Obama's proposal, it's not President Bush's proposal."

Obama called for tax cuts for the middle class, help for homeowners to stay in their homes, and help for local governments to build bridges and other infrastructure improvements to create jobs. Longer term, he said, he would expand health care and improve energy independence.

Turning to foreign affairs, the two clashed on Pakistan. Obama said that if Pakistani troops wouldn't go after Osama bin Laden, who's believed to be hiding in that country, then if U.S. troops had him "in our sights ... then we will take him out."

McCain said that Obama was threatening to attack Pakistan, and that would hurt relations. Obama countered that he wasn't calling for an invasion of Pakistan, but for getting bin Laden. As for speaking softly, he said that McCain was the one who had joked about "bomb, bomb, bomb Iran" to the tune of a Beach Boys song. McCain said he'd just been joking with an old veteran friend when he said that.

—Steven Thomma/
McClatchy Washington Bureau

Obama: McCain's negative attacks 'will not work'

Columbus, Ohio: October 10, 2008

Barack Obama today defended his character against mounting attacks from John McCain, daring his Republican opponent to run as negatively as he wants in the final weeks of the race while predicting that, in light of the financial crisis, "it will not work."

McCain's campaign announced a national TV ad that asserts Obama worked with a "terrorist" when it was politically convenient and then lied about their relationship. The man, William Ayers, is a professor of education at the University of Illinois at Chicago who in 1995 hosted a candidate event for Obama and was involved with two mainstream charitable groups in which Obama also had been active.

In the late 1960s and early '70s, when Obama was a child, Ayers belonged to the radical anti-war group Weather Underground, which advocated violence and placed bombs at the Pentagon and the Capitol. McCain's accusation is that Obama understated what he knew about Ayers' past or his beliefs when it suited him. There's no evidence that the two men are close or that Ayers has any connection to Obama's presidential campaign.

At a rally yesterday, McCain himself used the word "terrorist" to describe Ayers. Many participants chanted "liar, liar" when Obama's name was mentioned. At a rally this morning in La Crosse, Wisconsin, McCain seemed to dial back the tone. He didn't mention Ayers, and perhaps his most negative words were to paint Obama as "a Chicago politician."

"Nothing's easier than riling up a crowd by stoking anger and division," Obama said here, "but that's not what we need now in the United States. They can try to turn the page on the economy, they can try to deny the record of the last eight years. They can run misleading ads, they can pursue the politics of anything goes. It will not work. Not this time."

— Margaret Talev and William Douglas/
McClatchy Washington Bureau

McCain comes out swinging in final debate

Hempstead, New York: October 15, 2008

John McCain and Barack Obama clashed sharply in their third and last presidential debate tonight as McCain tried to paint his rival as insensitive to "Joe the Plumber."

McCain, trailing well behind the Democratic nominee in most national polls, was the aggressor, insisting that Ohio plumber Joe Wurzelbacher would pay more taxes under a President Obama. Obama insisted his Republican rival was too often ignoring the nation's economic issues and running an ugly campaign.

"One hundred percent of your ads, John . . . 100 percent of them have been negative," he said.

"That's not true," McCain replied.

McCain's recent ads have been negative; Obama has offered a mix of positive and negative.

Obama also repeatedly charged that McCain would simply continue the "failed" economic policies of President Bush.

"Senator Obama, I am not President Bush," said an annoyed McCain. "If you wanted to run against President Bush, you should have run four years ago."

That comment early in the 90-minute debate at Hofstra University set the tone for the evening.

There was much talk about the struggling economy — and that's how Wurzelbacher, a plumber Obama met recently in Toledo, Ohio, kept coming up.

"Joe wants to buy the business that he's been in for all these years," McCain said. "Worked 10, 12 hours a day. And he wanted to buy the business, but he looked at your tax plan and he saw that he was going to pay much higher taxes."

Obama said he'd cut taxes for 95 percent of Americans and raise taxes only on those making more than $250,000. In fact, he'd raise taxes on single filers making over $200,000 and couples making more than $250,000.

McCain called that "class warfare."

—David Lightman/
McClatchy Washington Bureau

Palin's rise to fame affecting Alaska image

Anchorage, Alaska: October 17, 2008

Like a sports celebrity or a high-end running shoe, America's snowy vacationland has a brand image to maintain. Since Alaska became regular headline fodder with Sarah Palin's vice presidential nomination, the state is everywhere.

Much of the buzz is the kind tourism experts like to see: Charles Gibson on the scenic shores of Lake Lucille. Wide panning shots of misty mountain vistas on CNN. Even a *Newsweek* cover with Palin holding a rifle over her shoulder reflects a desirable rustic charm. But, as the governor has become an increasingly controversial figure, some images have been less picturesque.

There was the national columnist who described Wasilla as "a soulless strip mall without sidewalks." And the parade of gory late-night jokes about aerial wolf hunting.

Unflattering comedy aside, Palin's rise seem to be good for tourism, said Ron Peck, president and chief operating officer of the Alaska Travel Industry Association. The governor's media prominence has sparked national curiosity about the state — more than 50,000 requests for information this year, double last year's count. The question now is how many of those will turn into real visitors.

Many Alaska boosters are looking at ways to use the press — positive and negative — to their advantage. Take Ketchikan, home of the infamous "bridge to nowhere."

"We made T-shirts," said Patti Mackey of the Ketchikan Visitors' Bureau.

One of them, made by a local artist, sat in a basket on the silent auction table. It read, "Nowhere, AK, 99901."

Then there's Cheryl Metiva, head of the Wasilla Chamber of Commerce. Woe to *New York Times* columnist Maureen Dowd should she ever cross Metiva's path. Dowd was the one who called Wasilla "soulless."

"She saw exactly what she was looking for and wanted to see," Mateva groused.

— Julia O'Malley/Anchorage Daily News

After drawing the biggest crowd of his fall campaign in St. Louis, Obama crossed Missouri to Kansas City, where an estimated 75,000 heard him on October 18, facing page. (Mike Ransdell/Kansas City Star)

Political, cultural factors fueling anger against Obama, analysts say

October 20, 2008

An ugly line has been crossed in this presidential campaign, one in which some people don't mind calling Barack Obama a dangerous Muslim, a terrorist and worse.

"To me, this all feels much worse than we've seen in some time," said Kathryn Kolbert, the president of People for the American Way, which monitors political speech.

Experts agree on the reasons: Obama, the Democratic nominee, is different from any other major presidential candidate in history in many ways, and people often don't accept such change gracefully. That different background fuels many fears, said Penni Pier, who's an expert on political rhetoric. People are still scared that terrorists are ready to strike and wonder about Obama's background, she said, while the Internet and other outlets are endless sources of misinformation.

Analysts see anger rooted in a number of societal factors, some cultural, some political.

"A great many people think they're about to lose power," said Mark Potok, director of the intelligence project at the Southern Poverty Law Center, which tracks hate groups. "The world is changing around them, and they can't stop that change. So their anger is boiling over."

The nonstop bile flowing toward Obama has been expressed in many ways.

At Becky's Cafe in Springfield, Ohio, Nicole Ratliff, a cable-television sales representative, echoed last week what many voters have said: "Obama won't salute the flag and he has said he was a Muslim."

Obama is a Christian and has never been a Muslim. The flag controversy erupted in September 2007, when then-fellow Democratic presidential candidates Bill Richardson and Hillary Clinton placed their hands over their hearts during the playing of the national anthem in Iowa while Obama stood with his hands clasped. An Obama spokesman said at the time that the candidate sometimes put his hand over his heart and had no substantive reason for not doing so.

The venom endures largely because not only is the Illinois senator the first African-American who's ever come this close to the presidency, but his background — biracial, lived in Indonesia for a time, grew up in Hawaii, has the middle name Hussein — isn't the stuff of past presidential resumes.

Angry voters have a 21st-century way to come together instantly and share misinformation. No longer do most people get news from newspapers or major television networks; instead they can access talk shows or Internet sites that are sympathetic to their own views.

"I can't recall a campaign where so many people held beliefs about a candidate that were demonstrably false," said Adam Schiffer, an expert on American political behavior and media at Texas Christian University, explaining what made these charges different from the standard campaign tit-for-tat.

Last week, a McCain supporter told the Arizona senator, "I don't trust Obama. ... He's an Arab."

"No, ma'am," McCain replied, "He's a decent, family man, a citizen that I just happen to have disagreements with."

— David Lightman/
McClatchy Washington Bureau

Hecklers waved signs and shouted during a Barack Obama speech at the University of Miami in Coral Gables, Florida. (Al Diaz/Miami Herald/MCT)

Final call to action on a somber day

Charlotte, North Carolina: November 3, 2008

"She has gone home...." Obama's eyes filled with tears as he praised his grandmother, who died November 2. He was at an election-eve campaign rally in Charlotte. (Jeff Siner/The Charlotte Observer/MCT)

At a personally bittersweet time, Barack Obama reached out to voters here today, speaking to thousands at an outdoor rally and personally calling a half-dozen from his local headquarters. He was on a final-day swing of a hard-fought 21-month campaign through three traditionally Republican states — Florida, North Carolina and Virginia.

"In these last 24 hours, we can't afford to slow down or sit back," he told a crowd at the University of North Carolina-Charlotte. University officials estimated it at more than 20,000. "Don't believe for a second this election is over. Don't think for a minute that power concedes. All of us are going to have to work like our future depends on it in the next 24 hours."

His visit on the eve of an historic election underscored how competitive the race was in a state that hasn't voted for a Democratic presidential candidate since 1976. Polls showed him essentially tied in North Carolina with Republican John McCain.

Obama gave the same stump speech he had delivered earlier in Jacksonville, Florida. But he deviated from his text to acknowledge the death last night of Madelyn Dunham, his 86-year-old grandmother.

"Obviously, this is a little bit of a bittersweet time for me," he told the crowd on the misty athletic field. "Some of you heard that my grandmother, who helped raise me, passed away.... And, look, she has gone home, and she died peacefully in her sleep with my sister at her side. So there's great joy as well as tears. I'm not going to talk about it too long because it's hard to talk about."

As he wiped away tears, he called his grandmother "a quiet hero."

"That's what America's about," he said, "and that's what we're fighting for and North Carolina, in just one more day, we have the opportunity to honor all those quiet heroes."

Last month, Obama took a break from campaigning and flew to Hawaii to be with Dunham as her health declined. The family said a private ceremony would be held later. At the university, Obama acknowledged what he called "incredibly gracious" condolences from John and Cindy McCain.

Earlier, during an impromptu stop at his storefront headquarters on Elizabeth Avenue, he greeted volunteers clustered into a room amid a throng of TV cameras and reporters.

On a day when his campaign canvassed neighborhoods and made last-minute calls, Obama personally telephoned several voters.

"This is Sen. Barack Obama, how are you?" he said to one.

"We need you to go out tomorrow," he told another. "It's going to be close in North Carolina. I'm counting on you."

At one point, Obama reached out to an elderly woman apparently overcome with emotion. Cradling the phone in one hand, he put an arm around tearful volunteer Alverna Bracy.

At his Charlotte headquarters, Obama left volunteers with a pep talk:

"I hope you guys feel like you're making a little history," he said. "We've just got to work 24 (more) hours. We can take North Carolina, and if we take North Carolina, we win this election."

— Jim Morrill/The Charlotte Observer

Victory

November 4, 2008

Barack Hussein Obama today was elected the 44th president of the United States, swept to victory by an anxious country eager to change course at home and abroad. Obama, 47, becomes the first African-American in U.S. history to win the presidency and the first from the generation that came of age after the turbulence of the 1960s.

His win suggested a new political order in the making. He drew masses of young people to politics for the first time. His biracial heritage reflected the changing demographic face of America. His mastery of the Internet matched the rise of a new information age. And his push into formerly Republican states in the South, Midwest and West marked a new political landscape possibly emerging.

After an epic struggle, the first-term Democratic senator from Illinois defeated Republican John McCain, 72, a hero of the Vietnam War and a four-term senator from Arizona.

"It's been a long time coming, but tonight, because of what we did on this day, in this election, at this defining moment, change has come to America," a triumphant Obama told a cheering audience of an estimated 125,000 supporters in Chicago's Grant Park, alongside Lake Michigan.

To those watching from abroad, he said that "a new dawn of American leadership is at hand. To those who would tear this world down — we will defeat you. To those who seek peace and security — we support you."

He lauded his wife, Michelle, and saluted McCain, calling him a "brave and selfless leader."

McCain conceded the election in a call to Obama at 11 p.m. Eastern time. Obama responded that he looked forward to working with McCain in the Senate.

"I need your help. You're a leader on so many important issues," Obama told him.

McCain then faced his disappointed supporters under clear skies outside a Phoenix hotel.

"The American people have spoken and they have spoken clearly," McCain said, his wife, Cindy, at his side. "I urge all Americans who supported me to join me in not just congratulating him, but offering our next president our good will and earnest effort to find ways to come together."

He also lauded his running mate, Sarah Palin, who would have become the country's first female vice president.

President Bush also called Obama shortly after 11 p.m. in Washington.

"You are about to go on one of the great journeys of life," Bush told the president-elect. "Congratulations and go enjoy yourself."

Obama was at the vanguard of Democratic gains across the country that promised him a solid working majority in both the House of Representatives and the Senate.

Eager for a popular mandate to reshape the government, Obama become the first Democrat to take a majority of the popular vote since Jimmy Carter eked out a 50.1 percent win in 1976. He won 53 percent of the vote to McCain's 46 percent. Obama sealed his victory by holding all the states that went Democratic in 2004, then picking off Republican states including Colorado, Florida, Virginia, Iowa, Nevada, New Mexico, Indiana and Ohio. Ohio was particularly important: No Republican has ever won the presidency without Ohio. No Democrat had won the White House without it since Kennedy.

There as everywhere, the faltering economy dominated voters' minds and tilted the political landscape solidly against the Republicans as the party of power — and responsibility — in the White House.

Interest was intense. More than 40 million Americans already had voted by this morning, and total turnout was expected to top 130 million. The turnout rate was likely to rival the modern record of 67 percent set in 1960, the highest since women were granted the right to vote in 1920.

President Bush, whose popularity plummeted after his close re-election four years ago, was all but invisible today, shunned on the campaign trail and watching the returns in the seclusion of the White House. He voted earlier by absentee ballot in Texas, where he expects to move after leaving office.

Flying home to Phoenix this afternoon, McCain and his aides sounded a sentimental note about the campaign.

"We've had a great ride, a great experience and it's full of memories that we will always treasure," McCain said as he spoke with reporters on his plane.

— Steven Thomma/
McClatchy Washington Bureau

The Obama family strode out to greet the crowd that gathered in Chicago's Grant Park on election night. Celebrating Obama's victory with him and his wife, Michelle Obama, were 7-year-old Sasha, holding hands with her father, and 10-year-old Malia, at her mother's side. (Chuck Kennedy/MCT)

November 5, 2008

Anchorage Daily News
Alaska

Merced Sun-Star
California

The Fresno Bee
California

The Modesto Bee
California

The Sacramento Bee
California

The Tribune
San Luis Obispo, California

Bradenton Herald
Florida

The Miami Herald
Florida

el Nuevo Herald
Miami, Florida

Ledger-Enquirer
Columbus, Georgia

The Telegraph
Macon, Georgia

Idaho Statesman
Boise, Idaho

Belleville News-Democrat
Illinois

The Wichita Eagle
Kansas

Lexington Herald-Leader
Kentucky

Sun Herald
Gulfport, Mississippi

The Kansas City Star
Missouri

The Charlotte Observer
North Carolina

The News & Observer
Raleigh, North Carolina

Centre Daily Times
State College, Pennsylvania

The Beaufort Gazette
South Carolina

The Herald
Rock Hill, South Carolina

The Island Packet
Bluffton, South Carolina

The State
Columbia, South Carolina

The Sun News
Myrtle Beach, South Carolina

Fort Worth Star-Telegram

The Bellingham Herald
Washington

The Olympian
Olympia, Washington

The News Tribune
Tacoma, Washington

Tri-City Herald
Kennewick, Washington

THE NEW PRESIDENT

At the Lincoln Memorial in Washington, the president-elect addressed thousands of people who gathered for the Obama Inaugural Celebration on January 18, 2009. (Brian Baer/Sacramento Bee/MCT)

Inauguration Day

Former President Jimmy Carter and Rosalynn Carter arriving. (Harry E. Walker/MCT)

Among the crowd on the Mall, Cecillia Hailey of Atlanta, foreground, cheered as Obama was introduced shortly before taking the oath of office. (Travis Heying/Wichita Eagle/MCT)

Edward Kennedy entered the dignitaries' seating area. (J. Scott Applewhite, pool/MCT)

From left, former President George H.W. Bush, Secretary of State-designate Hillary Clinton and former President Bill Clinton. (Chuck Kennedy/MCT)

Sasha Obama gazed up at her father. (Brian Baer/ Sacramento Bee/MCT).
Joseph Biden, right, took the oath as vice president. (Mark Wilson,pool/MCT)

Sworn in

Washington, D.C.: January 20, 2009

Obama took the oath of office from Chief Justice John Roberts on the west front of the Capitol. (Harry E. Walker/MCT)

Barack Hussein Obama became the 44th president of the United States today, a confident young leader ushering in a new era.

Taking the oath on the steps of a Capitol built in part by slaves, Obama became the first African-American to reach the pinnacle of American political life. He looked out over a sea of people sitting and standing in the cold, faces of every color creased with age and fresh with promise, celebrating a turning point of history and looking eagerly for a new voice and vision to lead the country in a new century.

"The challenges we face are real," he said in a 19-minute inaugural address that was at turns sober about the nation's problems and uplifting about its prospects. "They will not be met easily or in a short span of time. But know this, America: They will be met."

To his countrymen, he urged "a new era of responsibility." To the world, he vowed to protect American security without violating "the rule of law and the rights of man," and to talk even to hostile nations. "We will extend a hand if you are willing to unclench your fist," he said. To those who threaten the United States, he said, "you cannot outlast us, and we will defeat you."

The man he succeeded, George W. Bush, 62, watched quietly from his seat. At 47, Obama is the first American president who came of age after the turbulence and divisions of the 1960s and the Vietnam War.

Shortly after he became president at the stroke of noon, Obama placed his hand on the same Bible that Abraham Lincoln used at his 1861 inauguration and, following Chief Justice John G. Roberts, took the oath:

"I, Barack Hussein Obama, do solemnly swear that I will execute the office of president of the United States faithfully, and will to the best of my ability preserve, protect and defend the Constitution of the United States."

Obama paused for a second when Roberts placed the word "faithfully" at the wrong spot in the sentence, then repeated it as Roberts had, not as it was written into the Constitution more than 200 years ago, which is "faithfully execute the office."

He finished with the phrase that George Washington added and every president since has used voluntarily:

"So help me God."

His wife, Michelle, and his young daughters, Malia and Sasha, stood beside him, smiling broadly. Artillery hailed the man and the moment with a 21-gun salute that echoed through the marbled monuments. The ceremony was seen around the world, by American troops standing watch in such far-flung places as Afghanistan, Iraq and South Korea, and by countless citizens of other countries eager to see the new young president take power.

Among those attending were several of the nine African-Americans who, as children, needed the protection of National Guardsmen when they integrated Little Rock Central High School in 1957. Also among the honored guests were the surviving Tuskegee Airmen, the famed African-American aviators of World War II.

On the National Mall, children smiled and waved flags. Older Americans with memories of past struggles wiped tears from their eyes. They stretched shoulder to shoulder for the two miles that separate the Capitol from the Lincoln Memorial, where the Rev. Martin Luther King Jr. once spoke of the "dream" of such a moment when Americans would be judged by the content of their characters and not the color of their skin.

"We know today," said Rick Warren, a California pastor and writer whom Obama chose to give the opening prayer at the ceremony, "that Dr. King and a great cloud of witnesses are shouting in heaven."

— Steven Thomma/
McClatchy Washington Bureau

Facing page: The view from the Capitol down the Mall. (Mark Wilson, pool/MCT)

'The challenges we face...will be met'

January 20, 2009

This is the text of President Barack Obama's inaugural address as prepared for delivery.

My fellow citizens:

I stand here today humbled by the task before us, grateful for the trust you have bestowed, mindful of the sacrifices borne by our ancestors. I thank President Bush for his service to our nation, as well as the generosity and cooperation he has shown throughout this transition.

Forty-four Americans have now taken the presidential oath. The words have been spoken during rising tides of prosperity and the still waters of peace. Yet, every so often the oath is taken amidst gathering clouds and raging storms. At these moments, America has carried on not simply because of the skill or vision of those in high office, but because we the people have remained faithful to the ideals of our forbearers, and true to our founding documents.

So it has been. So it must be with this generation of Americans.

That we are in the midst of crisis is now well understood. Our nation is at war, against a far-reaching network of violence and hatred. Our economy is badly weakened, a consequence of greed and irresponsibility on the part of some, but also our collective failure to make hard choices and prepare the nation for a new age. Homes have been lost; jobs shed; businesses shuttered. Our health care is too costly; our schools fail too many; and each day brings further evidence that the ways we use energy strengthen our adversaries and threaten our planet.

These are the indicators of crisis, subject to data and statistics. Less measurable but no less profound is a sapping of confidence across our land — a nagging fear that America's decline is inevitable, and that the next generation must lower its sights.

Today I say to you that the challenges we face are real. They are serious and they are many. They will not be met easily or in a short span of time. But know this, America — they will be met.

On this day, we gather because we have chosen hope over fear, unity of purpose over conflict and discord.

On this day, we come to proclaim an end to the petty grievances and false promises, the recriminations and worn out dogmas, that for far too long have strangled our politics.

We remain a young nation, but in the words of scripture, the time has come to set aside childish things.

The time has come to reaffirm our enduring spirit; to choose our better history; to carry forward that precious gift, that noble idea, passed on from generation to generation: the God-given promise that all are equal, all are free, and all deserve a chance to pursue their full measure of happiness.

In reaffirming the greatness of our nation, we understand that greatness is never a given. It must be earned. Our journey has never been one of short-cuts or settling for less. It has not been the path for the faint-hearted — for those who prefer leisure over work, or seek only the pleasures of riches and fame. Rather, it has been the risk-takers, the doers, the makers of things — some celebrated but more often men and women obscure in their labor — who have carried us up the long, rugged path towards prosperity and freedom.

For us, they packed up their few worldly possessions and traveled across oceans in search of a new life. For us, they toiled in sweatshops and settled

On this day, we gather because we have chosen hope over fear, unity of purpose over conflict and discord.

the West; endured the lash of the whip and plowed the hard earth.

For us, they fought and died in places like Concord and Gettysburg; Normandy and Khe Sahn. Time and again these men and women struggled and sacrificed and worked till their hands were raw so that we might live a better life. They saw America as bigger than the sum of our individual ambitions; greater than all the differences of birth or wealth or faction.

This is the journey we continue today. We remain the most prosperous, powerful nation on Earth. Our workers are no less productive than when this crisis began. Our minds are no less inventive, our goods and services no less needed than they were last week or last month or last year. Our capacity remains undiminished. But our time of standing pat, of protecting narrow interests and putting off unpleasant decisions — that time has surely passed. Starting today, we must pick ourselves up, dust ourselves off, and begin again the work of remaking America.

For everywhere we look, there is work to be done.

Facing page: Speaking to the crowd and the country. (Brian Baer/Sacramento Bee)

The state of the economy calls for action, bold and swift, and we will act — not only to create new jobs, but to lay a new foundation for growth. We will build the roads and bridges, the electric grids and digital lines that feed our commerce and bind us together. We will restore science to its rightful place, and wield technology's wonders to raise health care's quality and lower its cost. We will harness the sun and the winds and the soil to fuel our cars and run our factories. And we will transform our schools and colleges and universities to meet the demands of a new age. All this we can do. And all this we will do.

Now, there are some who question the scale of our ambitions — who suggest that our system cannot tolerate too many big plans. Their memories are short. For they have forgotten what this country has already done; what free men and women can achieve when imagination is joined to common purpose, and necessity to courage.

What the cynics fail to understand is that the ground has shifted beneath them — that the stale political arguments that have consumed us for so long no longer apply. The question we ask today is not whether our government is too big or too small, but whether it works — whether it helps families find jobs at a decent wage, care they can afford, a retirement that is dignified. Where the answer is yes, we intend to move forward. Where the answer is no, programs will end. And those of us who manage the public's dollars will be held to account — to spend wisely, reform bad habits, and do our business in the light of day — because only then can we restore the vital trust between a people and their government.

Nor is the question before us whether the market is a force for good or ill. Its power to generate wealth and expand freedom is unmatched, but this crisis has reminded us that without a watchful eye, the market can spin out of control — and that a nation cannot prosper long when it favors only the prosperous.

The success of our economy has always depended not just on the size of our Gross Domestic Product, but on the reach of our prosperity; on our ability to extend opportunity to every willing heart — not out of charity, but because it is the surest route to our common good.

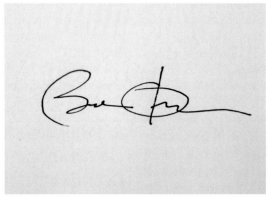

A proclamation bore Barack Obama's first signature as president. (Molly Riley/Pool/MCT)

As for our common defense, we reject as false the choice between our safety and our ideals. Our Founding Fathers, faced with perils we can scarcely imagine, drafted a charter to assure the rule of law and the rights of man, a charter expanded by the blood of generations. Those ideals still light the world, and we will not give them up for expedience's sake.

And so to all other peoples and governments who are watching today, from the grandest capitals to the small village where my father was born: know that America is a friend of each nation and every man, woman, and child who seeks a future of peace and dignity, and that we are ready to lead once more. Recall that earlier generations faced down fascism and communism not just with missiles and tanks, but with sturdy alliances and enduring convictions. They understood that our power alone cannot protect us, nor does it entitle us to do as we please. Instead, they knew that our power grows through its prudent use; our security emanates from the justness of our cause, the force of our example, the tempering qualities of humility and restraint.

We are the keepers of this legacy. Guided by these principles once more, we can meet those new threats that demand even greater effort — even greater cooperation and understanding between nations. We will begin to responsibly leave Iraq to its people, and forge a hard-earned peace in Afghanistan. With old friends and former foes, we will work tirelessly to lessen the nuclear threat, and roll back the specter of a warming planet. We will not apologize for our way of life, nor will we waver in its defense, and for those who seek to advance their aims by inducing terror and slaughtering innocents, we say to you now that our spirit is stronger and cannot be broken; you cannot outlast us, and we will defeat you.

For we know that our patchwork heritage is a strength, not a weakness. We are a nation of Christians and Muslims, Jews and Hindus — and non-believers. We are shaped by every language and culture, drawn from every end of this Earth; and because we have tasted the bitter swill of civil war and segregation, and emerged from that dark chapter stronger and more united, we cannot help but believe that the old hatreds shall someday pass; that the lines of tribe shall soon dissolve; that as the world grows smaller, our common humanity shall reveal itself; and that America must play its role in ushering in a new era of peace.

To the Muslim world, we seek a new way forward, based on mutual interest and mutual respect. To those leaders around the globe who seek to sow conflict, or blame their society's ills on the West — know that your people will judge you on what you can build, not what you destroy. To those who cling to power through corruption and deceit and the silencing of dissent, know that you are on the wrong side of history; but that we will extend a hand if you are willing to unclench your fist.

To the people of poor nations, we pledge to work alongside you to make your farms flourish and let clean waters flow; to nourish starved bodies and feed hungry minds. And to those nations like ours that enjoy relative plenty, we say we can no longer afford indifference to suffering outside our borders; nor can we consume the world's resources without regard to effect. For the world has changed, and we must change with it.

As we consider the road that unfolds before us, we remember with humble gratitude those brave Americans who, at this very hour, patrol far-off deserts and distant mountains. They have something to tell us today, just as the fallen heroes who lie in Arlington whisper through the ages. We honor them not only because they are guardians of our liberty, but because they embody the spirit of service; a willingness to find meaning in something greater than themselves. And yet, at this moment — a moment that will define a generation — it is precisely this spirit that must inhabit us all.

For as much as government can do and must do, it is ultimately the faith and determination of the American people upon which this nation relies. It is the kindness to take in a stranger when the levees break, the selflessness of workers who would rather cut their hours than see a friend lose their job which sees us through our darkest hours. It is the firefighter's courage to storm a stairway filled with smoke, but also a parent's willingness to nurture a child, that finally decides our fate.

Our challenges may be new. The instruments with which we meet them may be new. But those values upon which our success depends — hard work and honesty, courage and fair play, tolerance and curiosity, loyalty and patriotism — these things are old. These things are true. They have been the quiet force of progress throughout our history. What is demanded then is a return to these truths. What is required of us now is a new era of responsibility — a recognition, on the part of every American, that we have duties to ourselves, our nation, and the world, duties that we do not grudgingly accept but rather seize gladly, firm in the knowledge that there is nothing so satisfying to the spirit, so defining of our character, than giving our all to a difficult task.

This is the price and the promise of citizenship.

This is the source of our confidence — the knowledge that God calls on us to shape an uncertain destiny.

This is the meaning of our liberty and our creed — why men and women and children of every race and every faith can join in celebration across this magnificent mall, and why a man whose father less than 60 years ago might not have been served at a local restaurant can now stand before you to take a most sacred oath.

So let us mark this day with remembrance, of who we are and how far we have traveled. In the year of America's birth, in the coldest of months, a small band of patriots huddled by dying campfires on the shores of an icy river. The capital was abandoned. The enemy was advancing. The snow was stained with blood. At a moment when the outcome of our revolution was most in doubt, the father of our nation ordered these words be read to the people:

"Let it be told to the future world...that in the depth of winter, when nothing but hope and virtue could survive...that the city and the country, alarmed at one common danger, came forth to meet [it]."

America. In the face of our common dangers, in this winter of our hardship, let us remember these timeless words. With hope and virtue, let us brave once more the icy currents, and endure what storms may come. Let it be said by our children's children that when we were tested we refused to let this journey end, that we did not turn back nor did we falter; and with eyes fixed on the horizon and God's grace upon us, we carried forth that great gift of freedom and delivered it safely to future generations.

At the end of a luncheon inside Statuary Hall in the Capitol, the new president received a standing ovation from, left to right, Vice President Joe Biden, First Lady Michelle Obama, Speaker of the House Nancy Pelosi and Sen. Dianne Feinstein of California. (Lawrence Jackson, pool/MCT)

After the Obamas bade them farewell, above, former President Bush and Laura Bush departed Washington. Vice President Joe Biden and his wife, Jill, joined the Obamas, right, as the helicopter carrying the Bushes flew past the White House one last time, then turned past the Lincoln Memorial toward Andrews Air Force Base in the Maryland suburbs. From Andrews, the Bushes left for Texas in a jetliner no longer called Air Force One. Only the plane carrying the sitting president bears that name. (Above: Chuck Liddy/The News & Observer, Raleigh/MCT; right: Saul Loeb, pool/MCT)

The Obamas stepped out of their limousine and walked part of the way down Pennsylvania Avenue at the head of the Inaugural Parade. (Ted Richardson/The News & Observer, Raleigh/MCT)

At the President's Home States Ball, below, participants from Hawaii and Illinois raised cameras and cell phones to record the Obamas' arrival. (Corey Lowenstein/The News & Observer, Raleigh/MCT)

President Obama danced with the First Lady at the Commander-In-Chief Ball at the National Building Museum. (David Stephenson/Lexington Herald-Leader/MCT)

President Obama at work on his first full day in the Oval Office, January 21, 2009. (Pete Souza, the White House/MCT)

"...that we did no
we falter; and wi
horizon and Goo
we carried forth
freedom and del
future generation